SCIENCE RESOURCES

Developed at
Lawrence Hall of Science
University of California at Berkeley

Published and Distributed by **Delta Education**

542-0056
ISBN-10: 1-59242-997-1   ISBN-13: 978-1-59242-997-4
7 8 9 10 11 12 QUE 13 12 11 10 09 08

The FOSS year 2007 California Edition reflects significant contributions of dedicated professionals in the classroom, their students, administrators, parents, and concerned members of the scientific community. We acknowledge the thousands of educators who have given life to the ideas embodied in the FOSS program. We acknowledge and thank them all for their contributions to the development and implementation of FOSS.

FOSS Grades K–5 California Edition © 2007 Lawrence Hall of Science Team

Larry Malone and Linda De Lucchi, FOSS Project Codirectors and Lead Developers; Kathy Long, Assessment Coordinator; Teri Dannenberg, Developer; Susan Kaschner Jagoda, Developer; Ann Moriarty, Developer; Kimi Hosoume, Developer; Deanne Giffin, Early Childhood Consultant; Joanna Totino, EL Consultant and Professional Developer; Virginia Kammer, EL Consultant; Jaine Kopp and Jenny Maguire, Mathematics Consultants; David Lippman, Editor and Program Specialist; Carol Sevilla, Publications Design Coordinator; Rose Craig, Illustrator; Susan Stanley and Carol Bevilacqua, Graphic Production; Susan Ketchner, Multimedia Director; Alana Chan, FOSSweb Producer; Leigh Anne McConnaughey, Multimedia Artist and Designer; Dan Bluestein, Programmer; Roger Vang, Programmer; John Quick, Photographer; Alev Burton, Administrative Assistant.

FOSS Grades K–5 California Edition © 2007 Delta Education Team

Bonnie Piotrowski, FOSS Editorial Director

Project Team: Lynne Bleeker, Tom Guetling, Joann Hoy, Lisa Lachance, Elizabeth Luzadre, Paulette Miley, Cathrine Monson, Cyndy Patrick, John Prescott, Gary Standafer, Heidi Tyson, Nina Whitney

FOSS Grades K–5 California Edition © 2007 Content Reviewers

David M. Andrews, Ed.D., Professor of Biology and Science Education and Executive Director Science and Mathematics Education Center, California State University, Fresno, CA

Carol Balfe, Ph.D., Science Education Center, California State University of Fresno, CA

Ellen P. Metzger, Ph.D., Professor of Geology, San Jose State University, San Jose, CA

FOSS Grades K–5 California Edition © 2007 Teacher Reviewers

Amy Edmindson, Centralia School, Anaheim, CA; Amy Hellewell, Bonita Canyon School, Irvine, CA; Bonney Waters, Two Bunch Palms Elementary, Desert Hot Springs, CA; Christina Lambie, Highland Elementary, Richmond, CA; Debby Palmer, Turtle Rock Elementary, Irvine, CA; Heinrich Sartin, District 2 Office, North Hollywood, CA; Jeff Self, Washington Elementary, Eureka, CA; Jennifer Faulhaber, G.H. Dysinger School, Buena Park, CA; Jill Garmon, Brywood Elementary, Irvine, CA; Don McKenney, Oakland Unified School District, Oakland, CA; Jill Miles, Sheridan School, Sheridan, CA; Jim Jones, Valley View School, Coachella, CA; Joy Peoples, Riverside School, Riverside, CA; Katherine Jacobs, Verde School, Irvine, CA; Kathy Albrecht, Heritage Oak School, Roseville, CA; Lauren Vu-Tran, Fountain Valley School, Fountain Valley, CA; Lillian Valadez-Rodela, San Pedro MST, San Pedro, CA; Lori Van-Gorp, Anaheim Hills Elementary, Anaheim, CA; Maura Crossin, Local District 4, Los Angeles, CA; Melissa Tallman, College Park Elementary, Irvine, CA; Nancy Lester, Newport Elementary, Newport Beach, CA; Pamela Rockwell, Anaheim Hills Elementary, Anaheim, CA; Rhonda Lemon, Danbrook School, Anaheim, CA; Sherri Ferguson, Brywood Elementary, Irvine, CA; Susan Liberati, Beverly Hills School District, Beverly Hills, CA; Will Neddersen, Tustin USD, Tustin, CA

Production for California © 2007 and © 2003 Editions

LaurelTech Integrated Publishing Services

FOSS 1993–2003 Edition Staff and Contributors

Professor Lawrence F. Lowery, Principal Investigator; Linda De Lucchi, Codirector; Larry Malone, Codirector; Kathy Long, Assessment Coordinator; Leigh Agler, Developer; Susan Kaschner Jagoda, Developer; Kari Rees, Reading Consultant; Carol Sevilla, Graphic Designer; Rose Craig, Illustrator

Contributors: Sara Armstrong, John Quick, Eileen Massey, Joanna Totino, Denise Soderlund, Laura Loutit, Eric Crane, Yiyu Xie, Marco Molinaro, Susan Ketchner, Joannan Gladden, Lisa Haderlie-Baker, Sandra Ragan, Cheryl Webb, Alev Burton, Mark Warren, Marshall Montgomery

FOSS © 2000–2003 Delta Education Team

Mathew Bacon, Grant Gardner, Tom Guetling, Joann Hoy, Dana Koch, Lisa Lachance, Cathrine Monson, Kerri O'Donnell, Bonnie Piotrowski, John Prescott, Jeanette Wall

FOSS Grades K–6 Revision © 2000-2003 Teacher Associates
Claire Kelley, Dennett Elementary School, Plympton, MA
Dyan Van Bishler, Clyde Hill Elementary, Bellevue, WA
Sig Doran, Clyde Hill Elementary, Bellevue, WA
Ann Kumata, John Muir Elementary, Seattle, WA
Kate Shonk, Pleasant Valley Primary, Vancouver, WA
Theresa Fowler, John Rogers Elementary, Seattle, WA
Andrea Edwards, Woodland Primary School, Woodland, WA
Deanne Giffin and Janet Gay, Bancroft Elementary School, Walnut Creek, CA
Jill Kraus, Hawthorne Elementary School, Oakland, CA
Brenda Redmond, Los Perales School, Moraga, CA
Catherine Behymer, Napa Valley Language Academy, Napa, CA
Alison McSweeney, Dennett Elementary, Plympton, MA
Helen Howard and Carol Strandberg, Mt. Erie Elementary, Anacortes, WA
Rondi Peth, Dawn Mayer, and Jeannette Beatty, Fidalgo Elementary, Anacortes, WA
Virginia Kammer, Fresno Unified School District, Fresno, CA
Henrietta Griffitts and Jackie Meylan Dodge, Mt. Diablo Unified School District

Production for © 2000 Edition _FOSS Science Stories_
Creative Media Applications, Inc.
Rhea Baehr, Writer; Michael Burgan, Writer; Robin Doak, Writer; Matthew Dylan, Writer; Emily Lauren,
Writer; Matt Levine, Editor; Joanne Mattern, Writer; Dona Smith, Writer; Fabia Wargin, Graphic Design

Original FOSS © 1993–1995 Grades K–6 School District Partners
Kathy Jacobsen, Mt. Diablo Unified School District
Judy Guilkey-Amado and Alexa Hauser, Vallejo City Unified School District
Richard Merrill, Mt. Diablo Unified School District

Original FOSS © 1993–1995 Grades K–6 National Trials Center Directors and Advisers
Directors:
Ramona Anshutz, Kansas State Dept. of Education; Ron Bonnstetter, University of
Nebraska; John Cairns, Delaware Dept. of Public Instruction; Arthur Camins, CSD #16,
Brooklyn, NY; Winston Hoskins, Garland Independent School District, TX; Rhoda Immer,
Siskiyou, County Office of Education, CA; Mildred Jones, New York City Schools;
Floyd Mattheis, East Carolina University, NC; Alan McCormack, San Diego State
University; Don McCurdy, University of Nebraska; Joseph Premo, Minneapolis Schools;
John Staver, Kansas State University, Manhattan, KS; Brian Swagerty, Siskiyou County
Office of Education, CA; Sandra Wolford, Colonial School District, New Castle, DE

Advisers:
Sara Armstrong, Heidi Bachman, Carl Berger, Donna Dailey, Robert Dean, Steve Essig, Rosella
Jackson, Marsha Knudsen, Catherine Koshland, Samuel Markowitz, Glenn McGlathery, Margaret
McIntyre, Shirley McKinney, Richard Merrill, Marshall Montgomery, Gary Nakagiri, Karen Ostlund,
John Schippers, Dave Stronck, Dean Taylor, Judy Van Hoorn

FOSS © 1993–1995 Grades K–6 National Trials Leadership Partners
David Allard, Hal Benham, Diane Benham, Arthur Camins, Vicki Clark, John Clementson, Cathy
Klinesteker, Karen Dawkins, Sally Dudley, Sheila Dunston, Steve Essig, Fred Fifer, Theresa
Flaningam, Chris Foster, Robert Grossman, Cynthia Ledbetter, Charlotte McDonald, Karen Ostlund,
Janet Posen, Carlton Robardey, Twyla Sherman, Gerald Skoog, Dean Taylor, Mary Zapata

Published and Distributed by Delta Education, Nashua, NH 03063
The FOSS program was developed in part with the support of the National Science Foundation grants
nos. MDR-8751727 and MDR-9150097. However, any opinions, findings, conclusions, statements, and
recommendations expressed herein are those of the authors and do not necessarily reflect the views of NSF.

Science Content Standards for California Public Schools reproduced with permission, California
Department of Education, CDE Press, 1430 N Street, Suite 3207, Sacramento, CA 95814.

Physical Sciences
Table of Contents

Mixtures and Solutions

Life Sciences
Table of Contents

Living Systems

Investigation 1: Living Cells

Investigation 2: Vascular Plants

Investigation 3: Sugar and Cells

Earth Sciences
Table of Contents
Water Planet

Table of Contents

References

Mixtures and Solutions

Physical Sciences
Table of Contents

Mixtures and Solutions

PS1f. Students know differences in chemical and physical properties of substances are used to separate mixtures and identify compounds.

PS1g. Students know properties of solid, liquid, and gaseous substances, such as sugar ($C_6H_{12}O_6$), water (H_2O), helium (He), oxygen (O_2), nitrogen (N_2), and carbon dioxide (CO_2).

Mixtures

The next time you are at the beach, pick up a handful of sand. Look at it closely. You will see that each grain of sand is really a tiny rock. Not only that, the grains are different colors. And some of the grains are not rocks at all, they are little pieces of seashells. Sand is a **mixture.** A mixture is two or more materials together. This sand is a mixture of black, white, tan, and gray rocks, and bits of shell. A handful of sand is a mixture of several different things.

Sand

Mixtures are everywhere. But if you are not looking for them, you could miss them. The sidewalk is a mixture you can walk on. It is several sizes of rock mixed with cement. A bag of mixed nuts is a mixture you can eat. So are vegetable soup and carrot-and-raisin salad. And if you ate some mixed nuts, vegetable soup, and salad, just think about the mixture in your stomach!

Mixed nuts

Carrot raisin salad

Making Mixtures

Mixtures like sand or mixed nuts are made with two or more **solid** materials put together. Solid is one of the three common states of **matter.** Solid objects have **mass,** take up space, and have a definite shape and **volume.** A peanut, for instance, stays the same size and shape in your hand, on a tabletop, or in a glass.

A peanut stays the same size and shape in any container.

Chocolate syrup and milk is a mixture. Lemon juice and water is a mixture. So is oil and vinegar. These are examples of mixtures made of two **liquid** materials. Liquid is the second common state of matter. Liquids have mass, take up space, and have a definite volume. But liquids do not have a definite shape. A volume of water can have a different shape depending on whether it is in your hand, on a tabletop, or in a glass. Liquids are the shape of the container they are in.

Water changes shape depending on what you put it in.

Your breath is a mixture. The exhaust coming out of a car is a mixture. The air that surrounds Earth is a mixture. These are examples of mixtures made of **gaseous** materials. **Gas** is the third common state of matter, but we don't see gases very often. Most gases are colorless and **transparent.** Some gases, however, have color, like those that make smog. We can see air on a smoggy day.

A smoggy day in Los Angeles

Gases have mass and take up space, but they do not have definite volume or shape. A mass of air will not stay in your hand, on a tabletop, or in a glass. Gases are shapeless and expand to fill any closed container they are placed in.

Solids and liquids are often mixed. Salt and pepper are mixed with oil and vinegar to add taste to salad dressing. Flour and water are mixed to make bread. Cereal and milk are mixed for breakfast. Rice is mixed with water to cook it.

A breakfast mixture

Gases and liquids are mixed sometimes, but often the gas separates from the liquid as bubbles. That's what happens when you pour root beer into a glass. The carbon dioxide gas that was mixed with the liquid root beer forms bubbles. The bubbles rise to the surface and pop. Then the carbon dioxide in the bubbles mixes with the air. But for a while, the root beer is a lively mixture of liquid and gas.

A mixture of liquid and gas

Mixtures of solid and gas aren't often made on purpose. But they happen all the time by accident. If you fill a glass with marbles, you have a mixture of marbles and air. The spaces between the marbles are filled with air. The same is true of any solid objects in a container. And when it snows, the air is mixed with frozen (solid) water. Dust floating around in the air is also a mixture of a solid and a gas.

Can you have a mixture of solid, liquid, and gas? Yes. Remember that glass of root beer? Just add a few ice cubes. The glass of ice-cold root beer is a mixture of solid, liquid, and gas.

A mixture of solid, liquid, and gas

Mixing Solids and Liquids

Mixtures of solids and liquids are interesting. Several things can happen. When gravel and water are mixed, the gravel sinks to the bottom of the container. If you stir the mixture, things move around, but that's about it.

Mixing gravel and water

Mixing dry milk and water

Mixing salt and water

Gravel mixture after 5 minutes

Milk mixture after 5 minutes

Salt mixture after 5 minutes

6

When you mix **diatomaceous earth** and water, the powder makes the mixture cloudy white. After a while, the powder settles to the bottom of the container. When you mix powdered milk and water, the mixture stays cloudy white. When you mix salt and water, the salt disappears, and the mixture is transparent and colorless.

Gravel, powdered milk, and salt all make mixtures with water. After stirring, you can still see the gravel and milk, but the salt is gone. Salt is different in some way.

A mixture of salt and water forms a **solution.** When a solid and a liquid are mixed, the solid disappears into the liquid, and the mixture is transparent. This mixture is a solution. A solution is a special kind of mixture.

When the solid material disappears, it is *not* gone. It has **dissolved.** When a solid material dissolves, it breaks into pieces so tiny that they are invisible. When salt dissolves in water, it makes a saltwater solution.

Some solid materials dissolve in water and some don't. If a material dissolves, it is **soluble.** Salt is soluble in water. If a material doesn't dissolve, it is **insoluble.** Sand is insoluble in water.

The **solubility** of a material can help you identify it. For instance, if you have a white material and you are not sure if it is white sand or salt, you can put it in water. If it is soluble, the material is salt. If it is insoluble, it is sand.

Review Questions

1. **The three common states of matter are solid, liquid, and gas. How are they the same? How are they different?**

2. **What is a mixture?**

3. **Is milk a mixture, a solution, or both? Explain why you think so.**

PS1f. Students know differences in chemical and physical properties of substances are used to separate mixtures and identify compounds.

Taking Mixtures Apart

You made a mixture of gravel and water. It was easy. You just put 50 milliliters (ml) of water and a spoon of gravel in a cup, and the job was done. And you separated the mixture of gravel and water. That was easy, too. You poured the mixture through a screen. The gravel stayed on the screen, and the water passed through.

A screen can separate gravel and water.

All mixtures can be separated. But not all mixtures can be separated in the same way. The **physical properties** of the materials in the mixture can be used to separate the mixture. Particle size is a physical property of gravel. Particle size is a physical property of water. The particles of gravel are larger than the holes in the screen. The particles of water are smaller than the holes in the screen. The screen can be used to separate the mixture.

The mixture of diatomaceous-earth powder and water passed through the screen. The particles of powder and water are both smaller than the holes in the screen. What property will separate powder from water? Size again. Powder particles are larger than the holes in filter paper. Water particles are smaller. A filter paper will separate a mixture of powder and water.

Other Ways to Separate Mixtures

Imagine opening a kitchen drawer to get a rubber band. Oops, the rubber bands spilled. So did a box of toothpicks and a box of paper clips. The drawer contains an accidental mixture of rubber bands, toothpicks, and paper clips. How can you separate the mixture?

You could use the property of shape. You could pick out each piece one at a time. It might take 10 minutes to separate the mixture.

A mixture of paper clips, rubber bands, and toothpicks

Paper clips are made of steel. Steel has a useful property. Steel sticks to magnets. If you have a magnet, you can separate the steel paper clips from the mixture in a few seconds. Magnetism is a property that can help separate mixtures.

What about the toothpicks and rubber bands? Wood floats in water. Rubber sinks in water. The properties of floating and sinking can be used to separate the wood toothpicks and rubber bands in seconds. Drop the mixture into a cup of water. Then scoop up the toothpicks from the surface of the water. Pour the water and rubber bands through a screen. The water will pass through the screen, but the rubber bands won't. Job done.

Separating steel paper clips with a magnet

Separating toothpicks and rubber bands in water

9

Separating Solutions

A mixture of salt and water is a solution. The dissolved salt particles and the water particles are both smaller than the holes in filter paper. The property of size is not useful for separating a solution of salt and water. What will work? **Evaporation.**

Evaporation is the change of state from liquid to gas. Water evaporates, but salt does not. When a salt solution is left open to air, the water slowly turns to gas and goes into the air. The salt is left behind. Solutions can be separated by evaporating the liquid.

The salt left behind after evaporation doesn't look like the salt that dissolved in the water. Yes, it is salt. When the water evaporates, the salt reappears as salt **crystals.** Salt crystals always look square. Salt crystals often have lines going from corner to corner, forming an X.

Many solid materials dissolve in water to make solutions. When the water evaporates, the materials reappear as crystals. Each different material has its own crystal shape. Some crystals are needle-shaped. Other crystals are six-sided. And others are like tiny fans.

Sodium chloride crystals

Crystal shape is a physical property. Crystal shape can be used to identify materials. Whenever you observe square-shaped crystals in an evaporation dish, you will know that salt might be one of the ingredients in the solution.

Three different crystal forms

Review Questions

1. How would you separate a mixture of marbles, corks, and nails?

2. Would a screen be useful for separating a mixture of gravel and diatomaceous-earth powder? Explain.

3. Would filter paper be useful for separating a sugar and water solution? Explain.

4. Why does salt separated from a saltwater solution look different than the salt that dissolved in the water?

Summary: Separating Mixtures

What do fruit salad and hair gel have in common? They are both **mixtures.** A mixture is two or more materials together. Fruit salad is several kinds of fruit chopped up and put together. Hair gel is some sticky stuff and perfume put together.

Making Mixtures

On Earth, matter is found in three common forms, called states. These states are **solid, liquid,** and **gas.** Matter in any of its three states can be combined to make mixtures. A mixture can have solids, liquids, and gases all mixed together.

Some of the most interesting mixtures result from putting solids and liquids together. Sometimes solids seem to disappear when they are mixed with a liquid. This is what happens when salt is mixed with water. The salt **dissolves** in the water. This special kind of mixture is called a **solution.** Solutions made with water are **transparent,** that is, you can see through them clearly. If a solid is mixed with water and the liquid is not clear, like milk, the liquid is not a solution.

Some solids dissolve in water to form a solution.

Separating Mixtures

Mixtures can be taken apart. You can take fruit salad apart with a spoon. You can pick out the strawberries first, then the grapes, and finally the oranges. You can identify the strawberries, grapes, and oranges by their **physical properties** of color and texture.

Other materials have different properties you can use to separate them. Screens and filters can separate materials with different particle sizes, such as gravel and water. Iron materials can be separated with a magnet. Floating materials can be separated with water, and so on.

Solutions, such as salt water, cannot be separated with filters. The particles of dissolved salt are smaller than the holes in the filter. Solutions can be separated by **evaporation.** During evaporation, the water changes to gas and moves into the air. Salt does not evaporate, so it is left behind in the evaporation dish. The salt reappears as square-shaped **crystals.**

A salt crystal looks square and usually has an X from corner to corner. Other materials make crystals that are different shapes, like needles, fans, or triangles. The shape of the crystal can help identify the solid material in a solution.

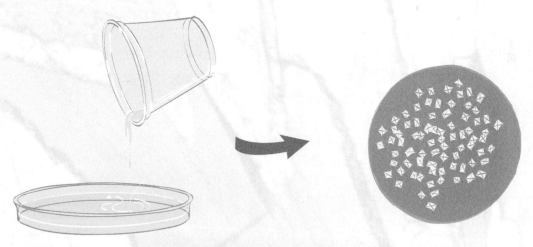

Solutions can be separated by evaporation.

Summary Questions

Now is a good time to review what you have recorded in your science notebook. Think about the investigations you have conducted with separating mixtures.

1. What is the difference between a liquid, a solution, and water?

2. What is a mixture?

3. What is a solution?

4. Is salt water a mixture or a solution? Explain.

5. Describe three ways to separate a mixture.

California Science Standards

PS1f. Students know differences in chemical and physical properties of substances are used to separate mixtures and identify compounds.

PS1g. Students know properties of solid, liquid, and gaseous substances, such as sugar ($C_6H_{12}O_6$), water (H_2O), helium (He), oxygen (O_2), nitrogen (N_2), and carbon dioxide (CO_2).

Vocabulary

mixture

solid

liquid

gas

dissolve

solution

transparent

physical property

evaporation

crystal

Extensions

Math Problem of the Week

Andy had a box of animal crackers. He counted them out and found 20 cookies: 7 elephants, 6 tigers, 5 monkeys, 2 zebras. Suppose Andy put all the animal crackers back into the box and took one out without looking. What is the probability of his choosing a. an elephant? b. a tiger? c. a monkey? d. a zebra?

Does the sum of the probabilities *a, b, c,* and *d* equal 1?

Home/School Connection

Make a mixture known as oobleck.

Materials
1   Mixing bowl and spoon
1   Measuring cup
•   Cornstarch
•   Water

Directions

1. Put about 1 cup of cornstarch in the mixing bowl.

2. Slowly add water to make a mixture, stirring as you go.

3. When the starch is all wet, it will turn into oobleck.

4. Explore the properties of oobleck.
   • Is it a solid or a liquid?
   • What happens when you place solids, like coins or spoons, on the surface?
   • Pick up a handful of oobleck. Can you hold it?
   • Can you cut a ribbon of oobleck with scissors?
   • What happens to the properties of oobleck when you change the amounts of the two ingredients in the mixture? More water? More cornstarch?

INVESTIGATION 2

PS1f. Students know differences in chemical and physical properties of substances are used to separate mixtures and identify compounds.

PS1i. Students know the common properties of salts, such as sodium chloride (NaCl).

Solutions Up Close

Salt solutions are transparent. You can't see anything in them. When you look at a salt solution with a hand lens, what do you see? Still nothing. In fact, you can't see anything in a salt solution even with the most powerful light microscope. Does that mean the salt is gone when it dissolves?

No, the salt is still there. To understand what happens to the salt, you have to think very small. You have to think about pieces of salt so small that it takes billions and billions of them to make a tiny salt crystal. We can call the tiniest piece of salt a salt **particle.**

Water is also made of particles. Water particles are different than salt particles, but they are about the same size. In liquid water, the particles are always moving around and over one another.

Let's imagine that we can see the salt particles. We'll represent one sodium chloride particle with this pink circle.

One tiny crystal of sodium chloride might look like this. The salt crystal is a solid. It has shape and occupies a definite volume.

If we could see water particles, they might look like this. The water is liquid. The particles are moving over and around one another all the time. That's how water flows. The mass of water has a definite volume, but water changes shape to fit its container.

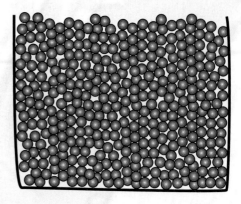

When you put a crystal of salt in a container of water, the salt sinks to the bottom.

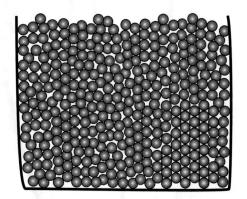

The particles of water bump into the salt crystal. This action knocks salt particles off the crystal. The loose salt particles become surrounded by water particles.

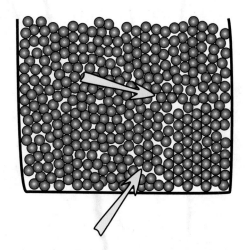

The salt particles are carried into the water. They end up spread evenly among the water particles. The particles of salt among the water particles are the dissolved salt. The particles of salt still on the bottom of the container are undissolved salt crystals.

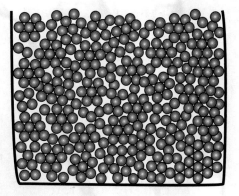

A solution forms when a **solute** dissolves in a **solvent.** The salt dissolves in the water. In this solution, the salt is the solute, and the water is the solvent.

Saturated Solutions

If you put one tiny crystal of salt in a bottle with 50 milliliters (ml) of water, the crystal will dissolve. You can imagine what the solution would look like at the particle level. There would be only a few salt particles among a lot of water particles.

If you add a spoon of salt crystals to the bottle, the salt will dissolve. Now there are a lot of salt particles throughout the volume of water. If you add ten more spoons of salt to the bottle, it will not all dissolve. No matter how much you shake the bottle or how long you wait, the salt won't dissolve. Why is that?

The solution is **saturated.** A solution is saturated when the solvent cannot dissolve any more solute. It's like there is no room for any more solute particles to fit in among the solvent particles.

If you start with 50 ml of water in a bottle, it will be saturated when about 14 grams (g) of salt are dissolved. If you put more salt in the solution, it will stay on the bottom of the container. The salt just will not dissolve. If you add another 50 ml of water to the bottle, it will take 28 g of salt to saturate the 100 ml of water. If you increase the volume of water to 1,000 ml (1 liter), you will find that it takes 280 g of salt to saturate the liter of water.

Supersaturated Solutions

Have you ever heard of rock candy? It is crystals of sugar. To make rock candy, you need to know some things about the science of solutions.

Sugar dissolves in water. It takes about 100 g of sugar to saturate 50 ml of water at **room temperature.** But if you heat the solution, more sugar will dissolve. The hotter you get the solution, the more sugar dissolves.

When the solution reaches its boiling point, it won't get any hotter. When you see undissolved sugar in the pan of boiling sugar solution, you know the solution is saturated. But there is about twice as much sugar dissolved in the boiling-hot saturated solution as there is in a room-temperature saturated solution.

A saturated solution at room temperature

A saturated solution at boiling temperature

A supersaturated solution at room temperature

What will happen to all that extra sugar when the boiling-hot saturated solution cools down? Will it stay in solution? Or will it come out of solution and pile up on the bottom of the container?

The sugar will stay in solution. A solution that contains more solute than it should is a **supersaturated solution.** When the boiling-hot saturated sugar solution cools down, it is supersaturated.

Now the solution is ready to make rock candy. When you roll a wet string in sugar, the sugar sticks to the string. After the sugary string dries, it is covered with tiny sugar crystals. Then put the string in the supersaturated solution. The extra sugar in the solution comes out of solution in the form of sugar crystals. The crystals grow on tiny sugar crystals stuck to the string.

The crystals will grow for a couple of days and then stop. Why do they stop growing? Sugar comes out of solution until the solution is no longer supersaturated. Then no more sugar comes out of solution.

Review Questions

1. **Explain what happens at the particle level when a solid dissolves in a liquid.**

2. **How do you know when a solution is saturated?**

3. **Sugar crystals aren't very big when they stop growing. How could you make bigger sugar crystals?**

PS1f. Students know differences in chemical and physical properties of substances are used to separate mixtures and identify compounds.

PS1g. Students know properties of solid, liquid, and gaseous substances, such as sugar ($C_6H_{12}O_6$), water (H_2O), helium (He), oxygen (O_2), nitrogen (N_2), and carbon dioxide (CO_2).

The Bends

Hard-hat diving was invented in 1861. The diver climbed into a watertight suit with a brass helmet. An air hose was attached to the helmet. Air was pumped to the diver walking around on the bottom of the sea 20 meters (66 feet) below the surface.

The **bends** is a condition that used to happen to deep-sea divers after returning to the surface. Divers felt dizzy, confused, and uncoordinated. They felt pain in their knees, hips, shoulders, and elbows. It became impossible for them to straighten their arms and legs. The pain caused divers to bend their arms and legs for pain relief. That's where the name *bends* came from.

The cause of the bends wasn't known until 1878. French scientist Paul Bert figured it out. **Nitrogen** bubbles in the diver's blood and joints caused the bends. But where did the nitrogen bubbles come from? To answer that question you need to know more about supersaturated solutions.

A solution is a solute dissolved in a solvent. We know about solids (salt) dissolved in liquids (water). Solutions can also be made when gases dissolve in liquids. That's what happens in the human body. Gases in the air that divers take into their lungs dissolve in the blood. Under normal conditions, the blood is saturated with dissolved nitrogen. No more nitrogen can dissolve.

When a diver goes under water, the pressure increases. Pressure compresses the air in the diving suit. The air particles are pushed closer together. As a result, more air dissolves in the blood. Air is 78% nitrogen, so most of the additional gas that dissolves in the diver's blood is nitrogen. After the diver has been under water for an hour, his blood is again saturated with nitrogen. But now it is saturated at high pressure, so there is more nitrogen in his blood than there was when he was at the surface.

Trouble starts when the diver rises to the surface. The pressure drops to normal. The blood is holding much more nitrogen than it normally holds at surface pressure. The blood is supersaturated with nitrogen. The extra nitrogen comes out of solution (the diver's blood) as nitrogen bubbles. The bubbles get stuck in blood vessels and stop the flow of blood. Bubbles form in the fluids in joints, causing a lot of pain.

The bends is **decompression** sickness. *Decompression* means changing from higher pressure to lower pressure. That's when the effects of too much nitrogen in the blood are felt.

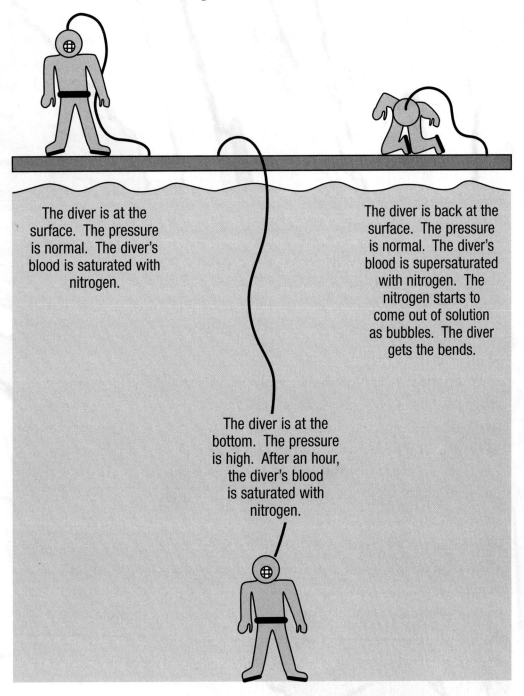

The diver is at the surface. The pressure is normal. The diver's blood is saturated with nitrogen.

The diver is back at the surface. The pressure is normal. The diver's blood is supersaturated with nitrogen. The nitrogen starts to come out of solution as bubbles. The diver gets the bends.

The diver is at the bottom. The pressure is high. After an hour, the diver's blood is saturated with nitrogen.

Decompression sickness also showed up in a different situation. In 1869 James Buchanan Eads began building a railroad bridge across the Mississippi River. The bridge needed support in the middle of the river. This required a lot of digging underwater. How could that be done?

Eads used **caissons.** A caisson is a huge box with no bottom. It is placed on the bottom of a river with the open side down. Air is then pumped into the box. The air pushes the water out under the bottom of the box. Now workers can dig and build foundations inside the caisson because it is filled with air.

The Eads Bridge

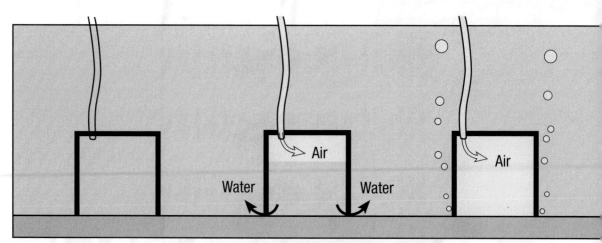

| The caisson rests on the bottom of the river. | Pressurized air pushes water out under the bottom of the caisson. | Pressurized air keeps water out of the caisson. |

The caisson was fitted with a tube that had tight-fitting doors. Workers climbed down the tube to the closed door at the top of the box. They closed a door behind them. Then they opened the door into the box. By using two doors, the pressure was maintained. This kept the water from flowing back under the bottom of the box.

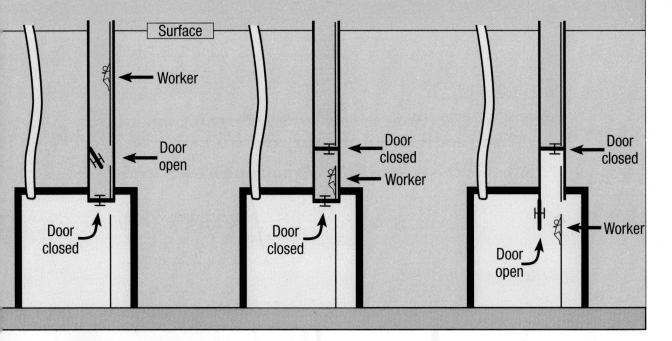

Areas where air pressure is the same as it is at the surface.

Areas where air pressure is high.

The problem was the pressure. The pressure in the box had to be kept high enough to keep the water out. The workers were breathing concentrated nitrogen, so more nitrogen dissolved in their blood. At the end of a workday, their blood was saturated with nitrogen in the pressurized environment. When they returned to standard atmospheric pressure at the water's surface, they had the same symptoms as deep-sea divers.

At a depth of 10 m (33 ft.) underwater, the pressure is twice as high as standard atmospheric pressure. The workers were in no danger working in the higher pressure in the caisson. The extra nitrogen in their blood did no harm. It was the change of pressure between the caisson and the surface that caused the extra dissolved nitrogen to rush out of the blood as bubbles.

Once the cause of the bends was understood, the condition was easily cured. Divers had to take more time to change the pressure back to normal. That meant coming halfway back to the surface and waiting there for 15 minutes. The nitrogen came out of solution slowly, so it didn't form bubbles. The extra nitrogen left the blood in the lungs and was exhaled. Then divers could come to the surface safely.

Review Questions

1. **What effect does pressure have on solutions where the solvent is liquid and the solute is gas?**

2. **What is the scientific explanation for the bends?**

Summary: Reaching Saturation

Substances are made of tiny **particles.** Every different substance has its own unique kind of particle. The water particle is different from the salt particle. The salt particle is different from the Epsom salts particle, and so on.

One particle of water, salt, or any other substance is too small to see. But you have to think about substances as particles to understand how things dissolve to make solutions. Here's what happens when you make a mixture of salt (sodium chloride) and water.

The salt particles are all stuck together. They form a solid crystal of salt. When a salt crystal is dropped into water, it sinks to the bottom.

Water is liquid. Water particles are moving around all the time. Water particles bang into salt particles on the edges of the crystal. The salt particles break free from the crystal and are carried away by the water particles. The salt particles get spread through the water particles.

When particles of one substance (a **solute**) spread evenly throughout the particles of a second substance (a **solvent**), the result is a solution.

If you keep adding solute to a solution, the solute will dissolve until the solution is **saturated.** A saturated solution is holding as much solute as it can. If more solute is added, it will pile up on the bottom of the container.

But if you heat a saturated solution, more solute will dissolve. In general, the hotter the solution, the more solute it takes to saturate it. A hot saturated solution has more solute dissolved in it than a cold saturated solution.

What happens to the hot saturated solution when it cools down? It becomes a **supersaturated solution.** A supersaturated solution has more solute dissolved in it than it should at that temperature. The extra solute will come out of solution as crystals until the solution is no longer supersaturated.

Gases dissolve in liquids to make solutions. Pressure affects how much gas will dissolve in a liquid. The greater the pressure, the more gas will dissolve. Carbonated drinks are saturated with carbon dioxide gas under pressure. When you open the bottle, the pressure is reduced. The solution becomes supersaturated. The extra gas comes out of solution as bubbles.

The same thing can happen to people, such as divers, who work in pressurized environments. Gases dissolve in blood. More gas dissolves when the diver is under water where the pressure is greater. When the diver returns to the surface, his blood is supersaturated with nitrogen. The nitrogen can come out of solution as bubbles, causing a serious condition called the bends.

Summary Questions

Now is a good time to review what you have recorded in your science notebook. Think about the investigations you have conducted with solutions.

1. **Describe what happens to a salt and water mixture.**

2. **How can you make a supersaturated Epsom salts solution?**

3. **How can you tell salt and Epsom salts apart?**

California Science Standards

PS1f. Students know differences in chemical and physical properties of substances are used to separate mixtures and identify compounds.

PS1g. Students know properties of solid, liquid, and gaseous substances, such as sugar ($C_6H_{12}O_6$), water (H_2O), helium (He), oxygen (O_2), nitrogen (N_2), and carbon dioxide (CO_2).

PS1i. Students know the common properties of salts, such as sodium chloride (NaCl).

Vocabulary

particle

solute

solvent

saturated

supersaturated solution

Extensions

Math Problem of the Week

A science class was doing an experiment to find out how much salt it takes to saturate 50 ml of water. Here are the class results.

Group 1 — 14 g   Group 5 — 15 g

Group 2 — 16 g   Group 6 — 12 g

Group 3 — 15 g   Group 7 — 14 g

Group 4 — 14 g   Group 8 — 20 g

Determine the mean (average), median (middle number), mode (most common number), and range (high minus low) of the class results. NOTE: A histogram might help.

Home/School Connection

Did you know you can make your own play putty? You will need

20 ml	White household glue (Colored glue won't work.)
15 ml	Borax
•	Water
1	Measuring cup
1	Set of measuring spoons
1	Spoon (to use to stir)
1	Plastic bag
•	Food coloring
2	Plastic cups or small jars (Baby-food jars work great.)

1. Mix 15 ml (1 tablespoon) of borax in a cup or jar with enough water to dissolve it (about 40–50 ml). This will make a saturated solution.

2. In a separate cup, mix 20 ml (4 teaspoons) of white glue with 5 ml (1 teaspoon) of water and a few drops of food coloring.

3. Add 5 ml of the saturated borax solution to the cup of glue.

4. Stir the mixture for a few minutes and watch what happens.

5. Test your play putty for stretch, bounce, and newsprint transfer. Store the putty in a plastic bag.

PS1a. Students know that during chemical reactions the atoms in the reactants rearrange to form products with different properties.

PS1b. Students know all matter is made of atoms, which may combine to form molecules.

When Substances Change

Tina made two solutions. She mixed citric acid and water in one cup. She mixed baking soda and water in another cup.

Tina poured the citric acid solution and the baking soda solution into an empty cup. Her older brother Leo opened a bottle of soda water and poured some into an empty cup.

The liquids in both cups bubbled and fizzed. Then they settled down to a slow, steady stream of bubbles. After 15 minutes, both cups were clear and still. The bubble show was over.

What happened in the two cups? Tina thought there was a **chemical reaction** in both cups. When you mix two substances, and a change occurs, the change is evidence of a chemical reaction. Tina saw bubbles in both cups. Bubbling is a change. Tina thought there must be reactions going on in both cups.

Leo had a different idea. He knew that the bubbles in Tina's cup were filled with **carbon dioxide gas.** But there were no carbon dioxide bubbles in the citric acid solution. And there were no carbon dioxide bubbles in the baking soda solution. The carbon dioxide bubbles formed only after the two solutions were mixed. The carbon dioxide was a new substance. A new substance is evidence of a reaction.

But Leo wasn't sure about the soda water. He didn't mix the soda water with any other substance. He just opened the bottle and poured. And up came the carbon dioxide bubbles. He didn't think the bubbles in the soda water were the result of a chemical reaction. But where did the carbon dioxide come from?

Carbon dioxide is dissolved in the soda water. The soda water is saturated with carbon dioxide under high pressure at the bottling plant. Leo released the pressure by removing the bottle cap. The carbon dioxide then came out of solution in the form of bubbles. Carbon dioxide was not a new substance, so there was no chemical reaction.

Atoms and Molecules

All matter is made of **atoms.** Atoms are the smallest particles that all matter on Earth is made of.

Ninety different kinds of atoms occur naturally on Earth. Some of them are common, and some are rare. You know the names of some of the atoms because they are also the names of common substances. Oxygen, hydrogen, iron, copper, gold, silver, carbon, calcium, and helium are the names of nine different atoms. A piece of iron is made of only iron atoms. A piece of carbon is made of carbon atoms. A helium balloon is filled with helium atoms. Ninety substances are each made of only one kind of atom. Atoms are the smallest particles of those substances.

Atoms can combine with each other to make new particles. Particles made of two or more atoms are called **molecules.** Molecules are the basic particles for most of the substances in the world. Molecules are created during chemical reactions.

One example of a molecule is carbon dioxide. The smallest piece of carbon dioxide is a carbon dioxide molecule. *Di-* is a prefix that means two. So *carbon dioxide* means "carbon two oxygen." The carbon dioxide molecule is actually made of one carbon atom and two oxygen atoms.

How Atoms Combine

We can make model atoms with circles and letters. Carbon will be an orange circle with the letter C. Oxygen will be a red circle with the letter O.

One carbon atom   One oxygen atom

When carbon and oxygen are heated, they react. The starting substances, called **reactants,** are carbon and oxygen. The ending substance, called the **product,** is carbon dioxide. Using model atoms, we can set up a **chemical equation** to show the reaction.

One carbon atom plus one oxygen molecule yields one carbon dioxide molecule.

Look at the reaction above. The number of atoms on the left side of the arrow is equal to the number of atoms on the right side of the arrow. Atoms are never created or destroyed during chemical reactions. Atoms only rearrange to form new substances.

Here is another example of a simple reaction.

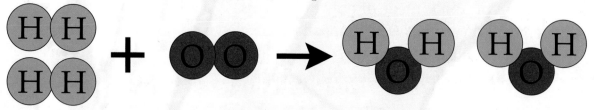

Two hydrogen   plus   one oxygen molecule   yields   two water molecules.
molecules

30

Two molecules of hydrogen and one molecule of oxygen are the reactants. Two molecules of water are the products. One water molecule is made of two hydrogen atoms and one oxygen atom.

Look at the hydrogen and oxygen on the reactant side of the equation. Two hydrogen atoms are touching, and two oxygen atoms are touching. Whenever atoms are touching, that means they are stuck together. Atoms that are stuck together form molecules. Because of their chemical properties, oxygen atoms are never found alone. Oxygen gas is always made of oxygen molecules. The same is true of hydrogen atoms.

Molecules are important. If atoms didn't form molecules, there would only be 90 different substances in the world. That's because there are only 90 different kinds of atoms. But atoms do combine to form molecules. And every different molecule is the basic particle for a different substance.

Look at the two molecule models below. They are made with the same three kinds of atoms. One molecule is the basic particle of common table sugar, called sucrose. The other molecule is the basic particle of citric acid.

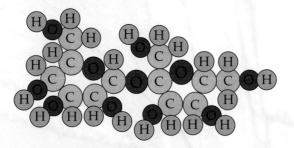

One molecule of sugar

One molecule of citric acid

The 90 different atoms and the endless ways they combine account for all the different types of matter in the world.

Review Questions

1. **What is a molecule?**

2. **What is an atom?**

3. **What happens during chemical reactions?**

4. **Explain how there can be so many different kinds of substances in the world.**

PS1a. Students know that during chemical reactions the atoms in the reactants rearrange to form products with different properties.

PS1b. Students know all matter is made of atoms, which may combine to form molecules.

Chemical Formulas

Sometimes people get a stomachache from too much stomach acid (hydrochloric acid). To feel better they take an antacid. *Ant-* is a prefix that means against. *Antacid* means "against acid." Baking soda can be used as an antacid. When the baking soda meets the hydrochloric acid in the stomach, a chemical reaction occurs. Let's see how that works.

Baking soda and hydrochloric acid are the reactants. Baking soda is a molecule made of one sodium (Na) atom, one hydrogen (H) atom, one carbon (C) atom, and three oxygen (O) atoms.

Hydrochloric acid is one hydrogen (H) atom and one chlorine (Cl) atom.

When baking soda and hydrochloric acid meet in the stomach, they react. The equation below shows the reactants and the products. The three thin arrows show where the atoms in the carbon dioxide product came from. Can you see where the atoms came from to form the salt and the water?

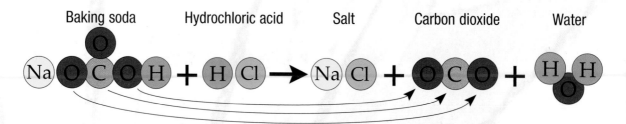

Count the oxygen atoms in the reactants. Count the oxygen atoms in the products. The number is the same, three. Count the other atoms in the reactants and the products. The number of atoms of one kind is always the same on both sides of the equation.

Using Chemical Formulas

One way to represent a substance is with its chemical name. Sodium chloride is the chemical name for salt. There is another way to represent a substance. It's called a **chemical formula.** A chemical formula is a code that tells *what kinds* of atoms are in a molecule. The code also tells *how many* of each kind of atom are in the molecule. The chemical formula for sodium chloride is NaCl.

Every kind of atom has a one- or two-letter symbol as well as a name. We already know the symbols for oxygen (O), carbon (C), hydrogen (H), chlorine (Cl), and sodium (Na). All the other atoms have names and symbols, too.

Remember oxygen? It never is found on Earth as a single atom. It is always attached to another atom. In pure oxygen, it combines with another oxygen atom to form an oxygen molecule. The chemical formula for the oxygen molecule is O_2. The little 2 (subscript) tells you that the oxygen molecule has two oxygen atoms. The chemical formula for carbon dioxide is CO_2. This formula tells you that one molecule of carbon dioxide has one carbon atom and two oxygen atoms.

Let's write the equation for the reaction of baking soda and stomach acid, using chemical formulas.

$$NaHCO_3 + HCl \rightarrow NaCl + CO_2 + H_2O$$

After the reaction, the baking soda and hydrochloric acid are gone. They have changed into new products. The new products are salt (NaCl), carbon dioxide (CO_2), and water (H_2O). Count the atoms in the reactants. The atoms in the products are exactly the same.

Review Questions

1. **Use chemical formulas to write the equation for the reaction between carbon and oxygen.**

2. **Use chemical formulas to write the equation for the reaction between oxygen and hydrogen.**

3. **What happens to hydrochloric acid when it reacts with baking soda?**

> PS1a. Students know that during chemical reactions the atoms in the reactants rearrange to form products with different properties.
>
> PS1b. Students know all matter is made of atoms, which may combine to form molecules.

Reactants = Products

Every substance is made of atoms. Iron is a substance. A piece of iron is made of only one kind of atoms, iron atoms. An iron nail is made of billions and billions of iron atoms. If you could break the iron nail into smaller and smaller pieces of iron, you would eventually have just one atom of iron. That's all there is to iron.

A Slow Reaction

You know what happens when a nail gets left outdoors for a long time. It gets rusty. Why is that? And what is rust?

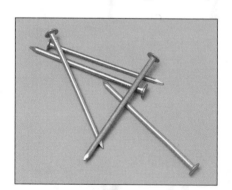

The iron in the nail reacts with oxygen in the air. The reaction produces new products. The rust is a new substance. Atoms of oxygen combine with atoms of iron to form rust. Rust is also called iron oxide. The chemical formula for iron oxide is Fe_2O_3. This is one way to represent one molecule of iron oxide.

To figure out what happens when iron rusts, a chemist writes a chemical equation. Chemical equations show how the atoms in the reactants rearrange during a chemical reaction to form new products.

The chemical formula for the substance iron is Fe. That means the basic particle of the substance iron is a single atom. The formula for oxygen in the air is O_2. That means the basic particle of the substance oxygen is a molecule made of two oxygen atoms.

With this information, you can set up a chemical equation for the rust reaction.

$$Fe + O_2 \rightarrow Fe_2O_3$$

Do you see a problem with this equation? When you count the number of iron atoms on the reactant side, you get one. When you count the number of iron atoms on the product side, you get two. Where did the extra iron atom come from?

To solve this problem, start with two iron atoms on the reactant side. Now recheck the equation.

$$2\,Fe + O_2 \rightarrow Fe_2O_3$$

The iron atoms are now equal. But the oxygen atoms are still out of balance. There are two oxygen atoms on the reactant side and three on the product side. Try starting with two molecules of oxygen on the reactant side.

$$2\,Fe + 2\,O_2 \rightarrow Fe_2O_3$$

Now you have two molecules of oxygen. Each molecule has two atoms. That makes a total of four oxygen atoms on the reactant side. But there are only three oxygen atoms on the product side.

Here's an idea. Start with three molecules of oxygen on the reactant side of the equation (for a total of six oxygen atoms) and two molecules of iron oxide on the product side. That should balance with six atoms of oxygen on each side of the equation.

$$2\,Fe + 3\,O_2 \rightarrow 2\,Fe_2O_3$$

Oops, the oxygen atoms balance, but the iron atoms don't. To balance the iron, you need to start with four iron atoms.

$$4\,Fe + 3\,O_2 \rightarrow 2\,Fe_2O_3$$

When an iron nail gets lost outdoors, a slow reaction takes place. Four atoms of iron react with three molecules of oxygen to form two molecules of iron oxide.

A Fast Reaction

Natural gas is an important energy resource in California. It is used in homes for heating and cooking and by power companies to generate electricity. When you burn natural gas, its chemical energy converts to heat. Burning is a chemical reaction. You can write an equation to understand how substances change when they burn.

A natural gas burner

Natural gas is mostly one simple **compound** called methane. A compound is any substance composed of two or more kinds of atoms. Methane is composed of one carbon atom and four hydrogen atoms, so it is a compound.

A model of one methane molecule looks like this.

A methane molecule

When methane molecules mix with oxygen molecules in the air, and you add heat by burning a match, a fast reaction takes place. The reaction gives off a lot of heat and light. And, of course, there are products. What are the products? Carbon dioxide is one product. What could the other product be?

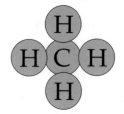

Hydrogen atoms could combine with oxygen to form water. One molecule of methane reacts with two molecules of oxygen to form one molecule of carbon dioxide and two molecules of water. The balanced equation looks like this.

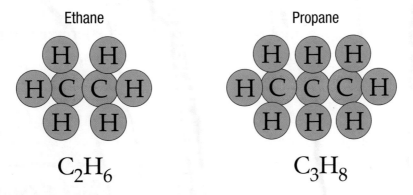

$$CH_4 + 2\,O_2 \rightarrow CO_2 + 2\,H_2O$$

Two other gases in natural gas are ethane and propane. The models and formulas for ethane and propane look like this.

Ethane

$$C_2H_6$$

Propane

$$C_3H_8$$

Do you see a pattern? Other molecules in the series are shown with their chemical formulas in the table below. Do you recognize the name of the eight-carbon molecule?

Molecule name	Number of carbon atoms	Chemical formula
Methane	1	CH_4
Ethane	2	C_2H_6
Propane	3	C_3H_8
Butane	4	C_4H_{10}
Pentane	5	C_5H_{12}
Hexane	6	C_6H_{14}
Heptane	7	C_7H_{16}
Octane	8	C_8H_{18}

Octane is an eight-carbon molecule. It is one of the main ingredients in gasoline. Gasoline is a mixture of many substances, but mostly it is hexane, heptane, and octane. When you go for a ride in a car, these three molecules provide the energy that moves you along. The equation for the burning of octane looks like this.

$$2 \, C_8H_{18} + 25 \, O_2 \rightarrow 16 \, CO_2 + 18 \, H_2O$$

Octane plus oxygen yields carbon dioxide and water.

Look at the products that result from burning two octane molecules. There are 16 carbon-dioxide molecules and 18 water molecules. Water is not a problem in the environment. But carbon dioxide is a **greenhouse gas.** Carbon dioxide is at the center of issues about **global warming.** California is a leader in looking for ways to reduce the amount of CO_2 released into the environment. That is why fuel economy and new sources of energy are important science and technology issues for all Californians.

Review Questions

1. **What information does a chemical equation provide?**

2. **Is rust the result of a chemical reaction? Explain.**

3. **Is burning methane a chemical reaction? Explain.**

4. **Write a balanced equation for the burning of propane.**

Summary: Fizz Quiz

Look around. The world is filled with wonderful and interesting things. Everything is made of one or more substances. Think about a market full of things to eat. And think of all the plants and animals you see in one week. Your clothes, schoolbooks, sporting equipment, phone, and medicines are made of different substances. All these things are very different from one another.

But all the millions of substances in the world are the same in one way. Everything is made of **atoms.** Atoms are the smallest particles of matter that combine to make substances. There are only 90 different kinds of atoms on Earth. But atoms combine to make **molecules** and **compounds.** Every different molecule is the basic unit of a different substance. All those different things in the market, your room, and the outdoor environment represent the many ways that atoms combine.

Atoms rearrange to form new substances during **chemical reactions.** You know a reaction has occurred when the starting substances, called **reactants,** change into new substances, called **products.** The new substances can be solid, liquid, or gas. And there might be additional evidence of reaction, such as heat or light.

The reaction between two gases, hydrogen and oxygen, to form water is an example of a chemical reaction. Two molecules of hydrogen and one molecule of oxygen rearrange to form two molecules of water. The reaction can be represented using atom models or **chemical formulas** in a **chemical equation.**

$$2\,H_2 + O_2 \rightarrow 2\,H_2O$$

Some reactions are slow. The change from iron to iron oxide (rust) is an example of a slow reaction. Others are fast, such as the explosion when a mixture of hydrogen and oxygen react to form water. But it is not speed that makes a reaction. The test of a reaction is that the starting substances change into new substances in the process. That's a chemical reaction.

Summary Questions

Now is a good time to review what you have recorded in your science notebook. Think about the investigations you have conducted with chemical reactions.

1. **How do you explain the millions of different substances found on Earth?**

2. **What is a chemical reaction?**

3. **What kinds of information do you get from a chemical equation?**

4. **What observations give evidence that a chemical reaction has happened?**

5. **What is the difference between a mixture and a compound?**

California Science Standards

PS1a. Students know that during chemical reactions the atoms in the reactants rearrange to form products with different properties.

PS1b. Students know all matter is made of atoms, which may combine to form molecules.

Vocabulary

atom

molecule

compound

chemical reaction

reactant

product

chemical formula

chemical equation

Extension

Math Problem of the Week

Rachel was interested in reactions that produce carbon dioxide gas. She wondered if there was some way to predict how much gas a reaction would produce. She did a series of seven experiments and measured the amount of carbon dioxide released by each one.

Baking soda (spoons)	Calcium chloride (spoons)	Carbon dioxide (milliliters)
1	1	800
1	2	1,600
1	3	1,600
2	1	800
2	2	1,600
2	3	2,400
3	1	800

1. How many milliliters of gas would be produced if 3 spoons of baking soda reacted with 3 spoons of calcium chloride?

2. How many milliliters of gas would be produced if 2 spoons of baking soda reacted with 1.5 spoons of calcium chloride?

3. Rachel wanted to produce exactly 2,000 ml of carbon dioxide. How much baking soda and calcium chloride should she use?

Home/School Connection

Baking soda (sodium bicarbonate—$NaHCO_3$) reacts with acid. One of the products is carbon dioxide (CO_2). You can use a baking soda solution to test common liquids, such as milk, tea, coffee, or orange juice, to see if they are acids. If CO_2 bubbles form when you mix the two solutions, the unknown probably contains an acid.

Materials
- Baking soda
- Water
- 1 Spoon (to use to stir)
- 1 Tablespoon
- Common liquids
- 1 Measuring cup
- 1 Small glass

Directions

1. Put 1 tablespoon of baking soda in the measuring cup.

2. Add water to the 1-cup level. Stir to dissolve the soda.

3. Put a small amount of the baking soda solution in a glass.

4. Add an equal amount of unknown solution. Record your observations.

PS1d. Students know that each element is made of one kind of atom and that the elements are organized in the periodic table by their chemical properties.

Organizing the Elements

Two thousand years ago, people were trying to figure out what things were made of. One idea was that everything was a mix of four basic properties: hot, cold, wet, and dry.

If you had just the right mix of hot and dry, that might make rock. A little less hot and a bit of wet might make wood. The right amount of all four properties might make a leaf.

Pure samples of the four properties were fire, air, water, and earth. These four substances were thought to be the elements from which everything was made. A table of the ancient elements looked like this.

Some people had a different idea about what things were made of. Chemists in the 1800s were busy experimenting with lots of different substances. They heated substances as hot as they could. They put acid on them. They ran electric currents through them. Sometimes the substances separated into new substances when they did their experiments. They then tested the new substances with heat, acid, and electricity. Some of the substances would not change any more. The unchangeable substances they called **elements.** These elements had different names than the ancient elements. The new elements had names like iron, copper, carbon, oxygen, hydrogen, sulfur, and gold.

Dmitry Ivanovich Mendeleyev

By the middle of the 1800s, about 60 elements had been discovered. A lot was known about them. Scientists knew about some of their **chemical properties,** such as what other elements they react with. They knew some of their physical properties, such as the weight of a standard sample of each element. When scientists made a list of the elements, they put them in order by weight. They started with the lightest element, hydrogen.

In 1869 a Russian chemist named Dmitry Ivanovich Mendeleyev (1834–1907) was writing a book about the elements. He made a set of element cards. Each card had the name of an element and everything that he knew about it. He put the cards in a row from lightest to heaviest, hydrogen to uranium.

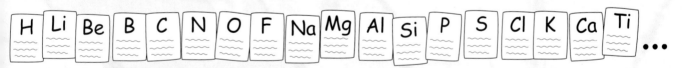

Mendeleyev looked at the long line of element cards and saw something interesting. The first two elements, hydrogen (H) and lithium (Li), had similar chemical properties. And as he looked down the line, he noticed that sodium (Na) and potassium (K) also had similar properties.

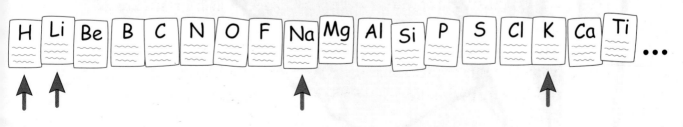

43

Then Mendeleyev saw that beryllium (Be), magnesium (Mg), and calcium (Ca) all had properties similar to one another.

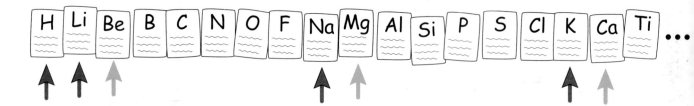

Mendeleyev had an idea. He reorganized the cards into several short rows. This way all the elements with similar properties would be in columns.

When Mendeleyev had all the elements laid out, he noticed something was wrong. For instance, the chemical properties of titanium (Ti) were not like those of aluminum (Al) and boron (B) above it. Titanium's properties were more like carbon (C) and silicon (Si).

When Mendeleyev moved titanium to the right, two things happened. The chemical properties of the elements lined up correctly. And there was a gap in the table of elements.

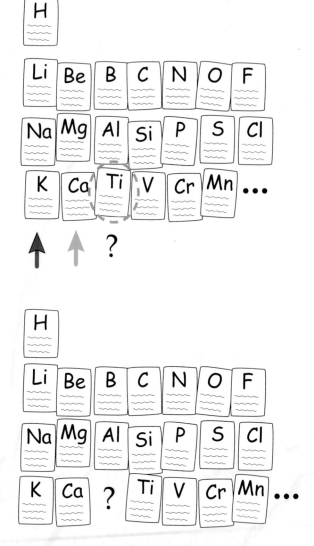

Mendeleyev looked at the gap and **predicted** that an undiscovered element must fit in that spot. Furthermore, he predicted the physical and chemical properties that the new element would have. In this way, Mendeleyev predicted about 30 unknown elements. Over the next 30 years, most of them were discovered.

The Structure of the Atom

About 100 years ago scientists figured out that atoms themselves are made out of smaller parts. All atoms are made out of the same three main particles. They are called **protons, neutrons,** and **electrons.** Protons have a positive charge. Electrons have an equal but opposite negative charge. Neutrons have no charge.

Protons and neutrons are clustered together in the center of an atom. This central core is the **nucleus.** Electrons are much smaller. They orbit the nucleus like planets around a star.

This is what a simple drawing of a lithium atom looks like. It has three protons and four neutrons in its nucleus. Three electrons orbit the nucleus.

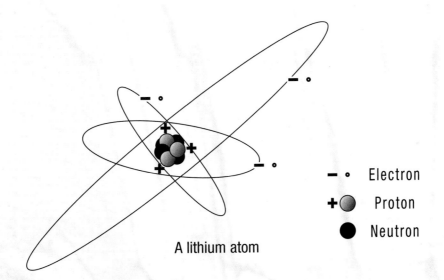

— °   Electron

+⬤   Proton

⬤   Neutron

A lithium atom

Remember, there are 90 different naturally occurring atoms, one for each element. But all atoms are made of the same three particles. What makes them different from one another? The answer is the number of protons, neutrons, and electrons.

The discovery of the proton in 1911 provided important new information about the elements. Experiments showed that the hydrogen atom has one proton in its nucleus. Hydrogen is the first element in the periodic table. The second element, helium, has two protons in its nucleus. The third, lithium, has three protons. Do you see a pattern? Uranium, the largest natural atom on Earth, has 92 protons. The number of protons in an atom's nucleus gave scientists a better way to put the elements in order.

The modern **periodic table of the elements** organizes the elements by **atomic number.** Atomic number is the number of protons in the nucleus of the element's atom. Mendeleyev's idea of putting the elements in rows so the chemical properties line up is still used. But Mendeleyev didn't know what we know today. There are only two elements in row 1, eight elements in rows 2 and 3, 18 elements in rows 4 and 5, and 32 elements in rows 6 and 7. This is the modern periodic table.

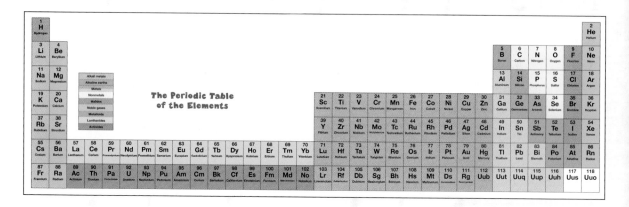

This layout makes the table very long. Often 28 of the elements are pulled out and shown below the others. Then the table fits better on a piece of paper.

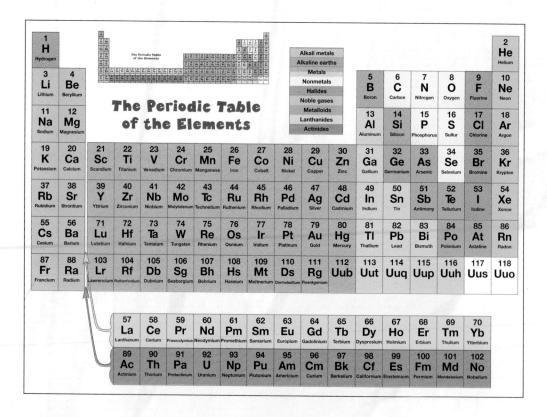

Color helps to show which elements have similar chemical properties. In the periodic table on page 46, elements that are orange, blue, lavender, and yellow green are metals. Green, red, yellow, and aqua elements are nonmetals. The green elements are called **noble gases.** They are interesting because they don't react with other elements.

There is a lot more to learn about the periodic table and the elements. In the next article, we will look more closely at the metals. Later we'll find out about the most common elements on Earth.

Review Questions

1. **How many different elements occur naturally on Earth?**

2. **How many different kinds of atoms occur naturally on Earth? Why do you think so?**

3. **How was Mendeleyev able to predict the existence of elements that had not yet been discovered?**

4. **What is atomic number? How is it used to create a periodic table?**

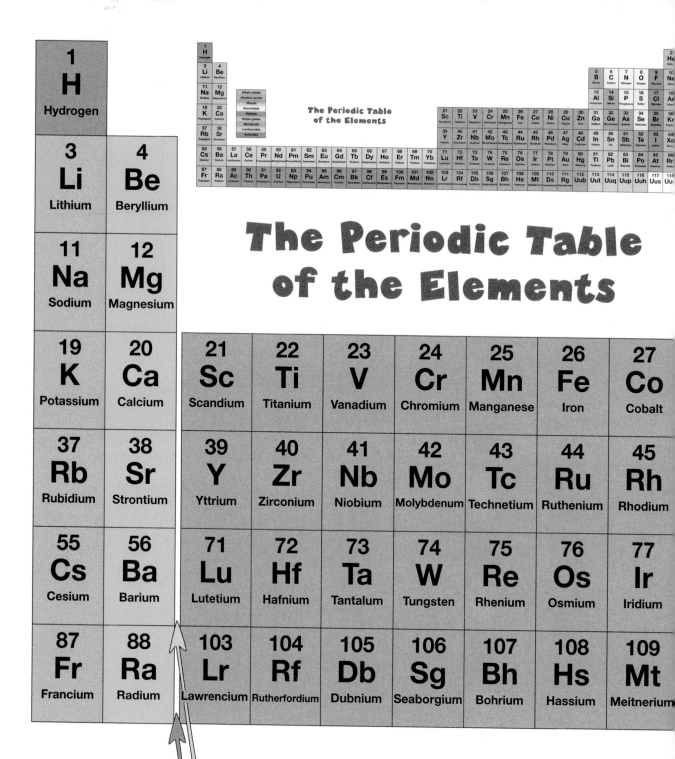

The Periodic Table of the Elements

1 **H** Hydrogen	

3 **Li** Lithium	**4** **Be** Beryllium
11 **Na** Sodium	**12** **Mg** Magnesium

19 **K** Potassium	**20** **Ca** Calcium	**21** **Sc** Scandium	**22** **Ti** Titanium	**23** **V** Vanadium	**24** **Cr** Chromium	**25** **Mn** Manganese	**26** **Fe** Iron	**27** **Co** Cobalt
37 **Rb** Rubidium	**38** **Sr** Strontium	**39** **Y** Yttrium	**40** **Zr** Zirconium	**41** **Nb** Niobium	**42** **Mo** Molybdenum	**43** **Tc** Technetium	**44** **Ru** Ruthenium	**45** **Rh** Rhodium
55 **Cs** Cesium	**56** **Ba** Barium	**71** **Lu** Lutetium	**72** **Hf** Hafnium	**73** **Ta** Tantalum	**74** **W** Tungsten	**75** **Re** Rhenium	**76** **Os** Osmium	**77** **Ir** Iridium
87 **Fr** Francium	**88** **Ra** Radium	**103** **Lr** Lawrencium	**104** **Rf** Rutherfordium	**105** **Db** Dubnium	**106** **Sg** Seaborgium	**107** **Bh** Bohrium	**108** **Hs** Hassium	**109** **Mt** Meitnerium

57 **La** Lanthanum	**58** **Ce** Cerium	**59** **Pr** Praseodymium	**60** **Nd** Neodymium	**61** **Pm** Promethium	**62** **Sm** Samarium
89 **Ac** Actinium	**90** **Th** Thorium	**91** **Pa** Protactinium	**92** **U** Uranium	**93** **Np** Neptunium	**94** **Pu** Plutonium

| Alkali metals |
| Alkaline earths |
| Metals |
| Nonmetals |
| Halides |
| Noble gases |
| Metalloids |
| Lanthanides |
| Actinides |

								2 He Helium

5 B Boron	6 C Carbon	7 N Nitrogen	8 O Oxygen	9 F Fluorine	10 Ne Neon
13 Al Aluminum	14 Si Silicon	15 P Phosphorus	16 S Sulfur	17 Cl Chlorine	18 Ar Argon

28 Ni Nickel	29 Cu Copper	30 Zn Zinc	31 Ga Gallium	32 Ge Germanium	33 As Arsenic	34 Se Selenium	35 Br Bromine	36 Kr Krypton
46 Pd Palladium	47 Ag Silver	48 Cd Cadmium	49 In Indium	50 Sn Tin	51 Sb Antimony	52 Te Tellurium	53 I Iodine	54 Xe Xenon
78 Pt Platinum	79 Au Gold	80 Hg Mercury	81 Tl Thallium	82 Pb Lead	83 Bi Bismuth	84 Po Polonium	85 At Astatine	86 Rn Radon
110 Ds Darmstadtium	111 Rg Roentgenium	112 Uub	113 Uut	114 Uuq	115 Uup	116 Uuh	117 Uus	118 Uuo

63 Eu Europium	64 Gd Gadolinium	65 Tb Terbium	66 Dy Dysprosium	67 Ho Holmium	68 Er Erbium	69 Tm Thulium	70 Yb Ytterbium
95 Am Americium	96 Cm Curium	97 Bk Berkelium	98 Cf Californium	99 Es Einsteinium	100 Fm Fermium	101 Md Mendelevium	102 No Nobelium

Element Finders

Sir Humphry Davy (1778–1829)

Sir Humphry Davy was born in Cornwall, England, in 1778. As a young man, he was studying to be a doctor. But his life changed when he picked up a book on chemistry. The descriptions of reactions and discoveries of new substances excited him.

Sir Humphry Davy

Soon Davy was conducting experiments in his small laboratory. Some of his first efforts ended in explosions. Others filled his lab with strange gases. Davy took a job working as an assistant for a chemist. One of the gases he discovered turned out to be nitrous oxide, or "laughing gas," a gas dentists sometimes use.

Davy's knowledge of chemistry grew. He took a teaching position at the university when he was 24 years old. He also became interested in separating compounds until they could not be separated any more. He used a battery called a **voltaic pile** to run electricity through a solution of potash. **Potash** is an impure form of potassium carbonate, K_2CO_3. The potash separated. Davy discovered the element potassium (K). People say that Davy actually danced around the room after this discovery.

Davy was one of the greatest element finders of all time. He is credited with more element discoveries than anyone else! Using his electricity methods, Davy discovered seven elements, including some you've read about. They are sodium (Na), magnesium (Mg), boron (B), potassium (K), calcium (Ca), barium (Ba), and chlorine (Cl).

Element Finders
Marie Curie (1867–1934)

Marie Curie with a glowing bottle containing radium

Marie Sklodowska Curie was born in Warsaw, Poland, on November 7, 1867. In 1891 she moved to Paris, France, to study mathematics, physics, and chemistry. After getting her degree in physics, she began looking for a subject to study for her doctoral degree. When she learned uranium gave off mysterious rays, she was interested.

Curie set up a small lab in the basement of the school where her husband, Pierre, taught. She studied X rays and other kinds of **radiation** from uranium ore. Curie thought that the amount of radiation coming from the ore samples was too strong to be only uranium. Curie discovered not one, but two new elements, polonium (Po) and radium (Ra), in the ore sample. The samples of radium she produced glowed with a continuous green light. She invented the term *radioactivity* to describe the radiation given off by the elements.

Curie was awarded the Nobel Prize in 1903. She was the first woman ever to win. She was awarded a second Nobel Prize in 1911, making her the first person ever to win twice! During World War I (1914–1918), Curie trained people to use X rays to find bullets in wounded soldiers.

Unfortunately, Curie didn't realize the dangers of radiation. In 1934 she died from an illness caused by exposure to radioactive materials. Her notes and laboratory equipment are still radioactive today, more than 100 years after she conducted her research.

PS1c. Students know metals have properties in common, such as high electrical and thermal conductivity. Some metals, such as aluminum (Al), iron (Fe), nickel (Ni), copper (Cu), silver (Ag), and gold (Au), are pure elements; others, such as steel and brass, are composed of a combination of elemental metals.

Metals

Look at the periodic table on pages 48–49. The elements shown in orange, blue, yellow green, and lavender are **metals.** That means most of the elements are metals.

Metals all share physical and chemical properties. They stretch and bend, but don't break when struck with a hammer. Most metals have shiny surfaces when rubbed or scratched. And all metals conduct electricity and heat well.

Pure metals are elements. When pure metals are found in nature, they are called native metals. Metals are usually found combined with other elements in rocks. Rocks that contain metals are called **ores.** Ores are processed to separate the pure metals. Metals in their elemental (pure) form have many uses.

Copper

Sometimes copper is found in its native form. More often it is processed from ore. Copper is widely used for electric wire and water pipes. It is used in more artistic ways, too. Did you know the Statue of Liberty is copper? The orange red copper changed to gray green over the years as the surface **oxidized.** When a metal oxidizes, oxygen from the air reacts with the pure metal to make a new molecule. The new molecule on copper is gray green.

Pure copper wire

Native copper

The Statue of Liberty is made of copper. Surface oxidation makes copper gray green.

Aluminum

Aluminum is one of the most common metals in Earth's crust. But aluminum is never found in its native form. It is mined as an ore called bauxite and turned into pure aluminum in a factory. It is then rolled flat and formed into thousands of products. Because aluminum is lightweight and tough, it is used for things like airplanes, backpack frames, car wheels, and cooking pots.

Aluminum is light and easy to shape.

Huge ingots of pure aluminum at the factory

Iron

The element iron is the backbone of industry. Naturally occurring iron is brittle. But when it is treated with heat and oxygen, and mixed with small amounts of other metals, it becomes steel. Stainless steel doesn't rust. Stainless steel is made by mixing melted iron with a second element, chromium.

Huge, strong structures can be made of steel. The railroad bridge shown below and the internal structure in the Statue of Liberty are made of steel. When iron and steel oxidize, rust forms. Oxidation slowly destroys the strength of steel, so steel structures are often painted to prevent rusting.

Native iron

Strong steel structures hold up a train bridge.

Precious Metals

The elements gold and silver are known as precious metals. These metals are rare. They shine with a bright luster when they are polished. They are found as native metals, but most often they are separated from ore. Over the years, these metals have been prized for artwork and objects of status. Gold, in particular, is used for jewelry because it does not oxidize when exposed to air. Gold and silver coins are highly valued as collectors' items.

Gold objects

Native gold

Native silver

Silver objects

Dr. Joaquin Ruiz

Joaquin Ruiz (1951–) was born in Mexico City, Mexico. After receiving a degree in chemistry, he worked with his cousin to figure out the age of the Mayan pyramids in Cacaxtla, Mexico. Ruiz's cousin was using a process called **carbon-14 dating.** Ruiz helped her find bits of wood and leaves that were trapped between the stones at the time the pyramids were made. They used chemistry to figure out the age of the pyramids by finding out how old the twigs were.

Dr. Joaquin Ruiz

Ruiz was excited about using chemistry this way. He went back to school and earned a doctoral degree in geochemistry from the University of Michigan. He then became a professor at the University of Arizona. Eventually he became the head of the College of Science. And he has continued using chemistry to figure out how old things are.

Ruiz studies how Earth formed. It's important to know the age of the rocks and minerals he studies. Ruiz uses radioactive elements like clocks to tell how old minerals are. Atoms of radioactive elements slowly change as time passes. Using an instrument that he helped invent, Ruiz can analyze the radioactive elements to determine the age of the minerals.

Using this instrument, Ruiz and a group of scientists figured out when and where the world's largest gold field formed. The gold is over 3 billion years old! Now Ruiz is working on another question. Why is copper ore concentrated in the western United States? What conditions created the copper-rich minerals? Where did they form? To find out, Ruiz must be part geologist, part chemist, and part detective.

Alloys

Mixtures of metals are called **alloys.** Alloys have properties that are different from the properties of the original metals.

Different kinds of steel are made by adding small amounts of other elemental metals to iron. Each kind of steel has different properties. Chromium is added to iron to make stainless steel, which doesn't rust. Nickel is added to iron to make nickel steel, which is tough and flexible.

Some alloys have unique properties. Aluminum, nickel, and cobalt are combined to make alnico, a strongly magnetic metal.

Copper is mixed with zinc to make brass. Brass has a golden luster. It is suited for use outdoors because it resists oxidation. Copper is mixed with tin to make bronze. Bronze is a tougher, more weather-resistant metal than copper or tin alone.

Native copper

Native zinc

Brass containers and key rings

Bronze sculpture outdoors in a park

Native copper

Pure tin

What Are Salts?

When most metals are put into acid, a reaction occurs. The metal dissolves and new substances form. The new substances are called **salts.** Most salts dissolve in water. Water containing dissolved salts conducts electricity.

Common table salt is sodium chloride (NaCl). It can be made by dissolving the metal sodium in hydrochloric acid. The equation for the reaction looks like this.

$$2\,Na + 2\,HCl \rightarrow 2\,NaCl + H_2$$

Sodium plus hydrochloric acid yields sodium chloride plus hydrogen gas.

Sodium chloride crystals

Other salts can be made by dissolving copper, iron, calcium, or zinc in acid. Chemists use salts in their reactions to create new molecules for medicines, building materials, and fabrics.

Review Questions

1. **What is an alloy?**

2. **What properties do all metals have in common?**

3. **Which of these metals are elements? Which are alloys? Nickel, bronze, steel, cobalt, chromium, alnico, gold, zinc, tin, brass.**

PS1h. Students know living organisms and most materials are composed of just a few elements.

Earth Elements

About 5 billion years ago, a huge star exploded. The blast sent a giant cloud of gas and dust into space. Over the next few millions of years, gravity pulled the bits of gas and dust closer together. Finally, the tiny particles formed the Solar System. The Sun, the planets, and everything on them came from that space cloud. Everything in the world, including you, is made of stardust.

What was that stardust made of? Elements. Atoms of all 90 naturally occurring elements were flying around in that space cloud. And when Earth formed, all 90 elements became part of our planet.

The Chemistry of Life

You are made of elements in the periodic table. How many of the 90 elements do you think it takes to make a person?

You probably have a trace amount of every element in your body. That's because elements are found everywhere, including our air, water, and food. For instance, helium is in the air in tiny amounts. Small amounts of helium enter our bodies when we breathe. We don't need helium to survive. But other elements are essential for life. We need tiny amounts of some elements, like chlorine and iodine. But we need large amounts of others, such as carbon and oxygen.

The human body is about 75% water. Water is made from the elements hydrogen and oxygen.

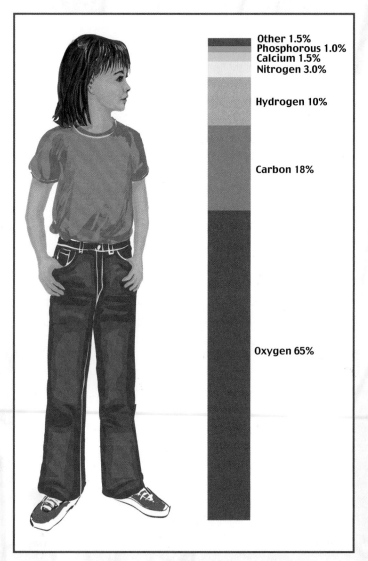

Other 1.5%
Phosphorous 1.0%
Calcium 1.5%
Nitrogen 3.0%

Hydrogen 10%

Carbon 18%

Oxygen 65%

Much of the rest of the body is made from the element carbon combined with oxygen and hydrogen. These three elements form **carbohydrates** (sugars and starches), **lipids** (oils and fats), and **proteins.** Proteins also contain nitrogen. The soft parts of the body, such as skin, muscle, fat, and organs, are made of carbohydrates, lipids, and proteins.

The tough, rigid parts of the body, like teeth, bones, and cartilage, are rich in calcium. Blood contains a lot of iron. Potassium and sodium are needed for nerve and brain function.

When you add it all up, about 98.5% of the human body is composed of only six elements: oxygen, carbon, hydrogen, nitrogen, calcium, and phosphorus. The remaining 1.5% is small amounts of a lot of different elements.

Most living organisms are chemically very similar to humans. So it's pretty safe to say that all life is based on the same six elements. And anything we use that comes from organisms, such as wood, paper, cotton, fabrics, plastics, food, and fuels, is also made of these six elements.

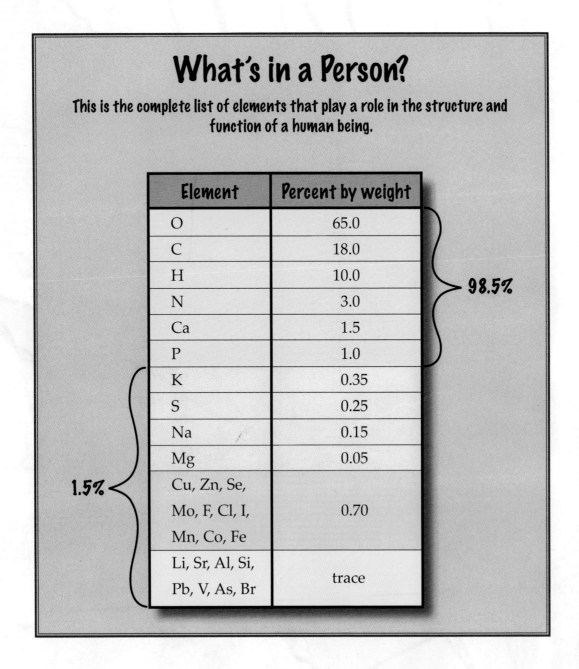

What's in a Person?

This is the complete list of elements that play a role in the structure and function of a human being.

Element	Percent by weight	
O	65.0	⎫
C	18.0	
H	10.0	
N	3.0	**98.5%**
Ca	1.5	
P	1.0	⎭
K	0.35	⎫
S	0.25	
Na	0.15	
Mg	0.05	**1.5%**
Cu, Zn, Se, Mo, F, Cl, I, Mn, Co, Fe	0.70	
Li, Sr, Al, Si, Pb, V, As, Br	trace	⎭

The Chemistry of Earth

Earth itself is made of elements. The most abundant element is iron (35%). The massive core of the planet is mostly iron. Next are oxygen (28%), magnesium (17%), and silicon (13%). These three elements are the main elements in minerals and rocks. They make up the largest part of the planet, the mantle and crust.

The other major elements that make up Earth are nickel (2.7%), sulfur (2.7%), calcium (0.6%), and aluminum (0.4%). The remaining 82 elements together make up a tiny 0.6% of Earth. This includes the oceans and atmosphere.

It might seem that Earth is a pretty simple place. It's made mostly out of a dozen or so elements. But Earth is not a simple place. It is not the number of different elements that determines how complex things are. It's the ways the elements combine to make molecules. These few elements can combine to make millions of different materials. That's where the wonderful variety on Earth comes from.

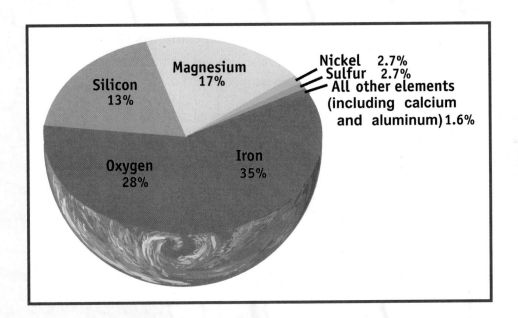

Review Questions

1. **What are the six most abundant elements in living organisms? What percentage of an organism is made of these six elements?**

2. **What are the six most abundant elements in the earth? What percentage of Earth is made of these six elements?**

3. **How can so many different substances in the world be made of so few elements?**

4. **What does it mean when a person says everything is made of stardust?**

PS1d. Students know that each element is made of one kind of atom and that the elements are organized in the periodic table by their chemical properties.

PS1e. Students know scientists have developed instruments that can create discrete images of atoms and molecules that show that the atoms and molecules often occur in well-ordered arrays.

New Technologies

In 1907 Ernest Rutherford (1871–1937) discovered the structure of the gold atom. His experiments suggested a solid positively charged nucleus with negatively charged electrons orbiting it. That was a breakthrough.

Using Rutherford's ideas, scientists were able to figure out the structure of all the atoms. With models for structures of the atoms, scientists could predict how atoms might combine to form molecules of substances. They predicted that atoms would arrange in **well-ordered arrays.** Well-ordered arrays are repeating patterns, like marbles in a box or oranges carefully stacked at the market.

For years it was impossible to find out if the predictions were right. Atoms were way too small to see, even with the world's most powerful microscopes.

A researcher with a scanning tunneling microscope (STM)

That changed in 1981 when a new kind of microscope was invented. The **scanning tunneling microscope (STM)** could create images of individual atoms! For the first time, scientists could see that atoms did arrange themselves in orderly arrays, just as they had predicted. Each white dot in the image to the right is one atom of silicon. The silicon atoms form an interesting pattern of circles.

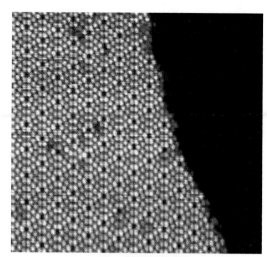

Silicon atoms in a silicon crystal

The Search for New Atoms

By 1930 all 90 naturally occurring elements had been discovered and described. The periodic table went from element number 1, hydrogen, to element number 92, uranium. Elements number 43 and 61 had not been discovered. They just didn't seem to exist on Earth. And no elements existed beyond number 92, uranium.

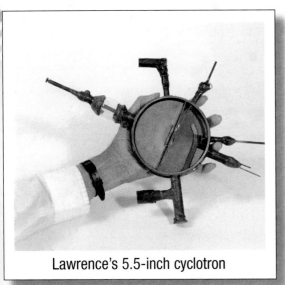
Lawrence's 5.5-inch cyclotron

Scientists knew that if they could put one more proton in the nucleus of a uranium atom, the result would be a new element, element number 93. But how could they do that?

In 1931 a young professor at the University of California at Berkeley, Ernest O. Lawrence (1901–1958), invented an instrument called the **cyclotron.** The cyclotron was the tool that made it possible to create new elements.

The cyclotron used electricity to accelerate protons and other atomic particles. The particles would move so fast that they would crash into the nucleus of uranium and stick there. In 1940 the cyclotron was used to make element number 93, neptunium.

Between 1940 and 1974, elements 93 through 106 were created in the labs at Berkeley. The work was done by teams, but two scientists provided leadership. They were Glenn Seaborg (1912–1999) and Albert Ghiorso (1915–). Not only did they decide which atoms to collide to make new elements, they had to design bigger and bigger cyclotrons. By the 1970s the cyclotrons were huge buildings.

Glenn Seaborg (left) and Albert Ghiorso

One of several particle accelerators at Berkeley

James Harris

(1932–)

In 1969 James Harris was a member of the team of scientists who discovered elements 104 and 105. He was the first African American scientist to discover new elements. Harris designed the part of the experimental system called the target. The target is necessary to identify the products of the high-energy collisions that produce new elements.

In the 1980s and 1990s, elements 107–112 were discovered. The work was done in Germany at the Heavy Ion Research Lab. The creations of elements 113–116 have been reported. The work was done in Russia by international teams of scientists. The discoveries have not been confirmed yet. It may be years before the experiments are repeated by other scientists to prove that the elements really exist.

Recently scientists at the Berkeley lab announced the discovery of elements 117 and 118. After failing to confirm the discovery, the scientists withdrew their claim. But pay attention to the science news. In a few years, you might hear about the discovery of element 120. Do you think there is a limit to the size of atoms scientists can make?

Lawrence Hall of Science, dedicated in 1968

Ernest O. Lawrence

The discovery of 26 transuranium (beyond uranium) elements has been possible because of the cyclotron invented by Lawrence. His tiny cyclotron started a whole new branch of science. During his 57 years, he accomplished a lot. He received the Nobel Prize in 1939, making him the first person at the University of California to be awarded a Nobel Prize. Two research laboratories are named for him.

After his death, Lawrence's family and fellow scientists wanted to build a memorial in his honor. They decided to build a science museum. It is the Lawrence Hall of Science. Every year thousands of families and school classes visit the museum. The Lawrence Hall of Science is an active, ever-changing science experience. It is a fitting memorial to a man who started a science revolution.

Review Questions

1. **How do scientists know that atoms and molecules combine in well-ordered arrays?**

2. **Explain why the periodic table has over 110 elements when only 90 occur naturally on Earth.**

Ask a Chemist

Angelica Stacy

Beryl Baker and friend

Beryl Baker's teacher asked her fifth-grade students to do a career report for an assignment. Beryl decided to do her report on a chemist's career. To find out what chemists do, she made an appointment to talk with Angelica Stacy, professor of chemistry at the University of California at Berkeley. Beryl had this interview with Professor Stacy.

BB: We are studying mixtures and solutions in our class. My teacher said people who work with mixtures and solutions are called chemists. What does it mean to be a chemist, and what does a chemist do?

AS: That's a good question. Chemists do study mixtures and solutions, but they also study all other forms of matter, including gases and solids. We study their properties and try to find out why they do what they do. We then use that information to make new things. Chemists make many of the things around you. The material of your jacket, the dye in your jeans, medicines, plastics, and lots more.

BB: Why do you like chemistry?

AS: It's more that I like science, and chemistry is one piece of science. For me, chemistry is a way of thinking about the world and contributing to society at the same time.

BB: Was there a person who started you thinking about chemistry?

AS: My father. He was an engineer with RCA. He never got a college degree because his family was poor, so he taught himself most of what he needed to know. Because of him, there was always science in our house. He was always making things that interested me, and talking about how sound and electricity worked.

BB: How long did you go to college to learn about chemistry?

AS: Four years of college as an undergraduate to get my bachelor's degree, and then 4 years of graduate work to get the advanced degree so I could become a professor. In my case, it took 8 years of college-level study.

BB: Do all chemists work at colleges or universities?

AS: No. There is a big chemical industry worldwide. One [industry] that you probably know about is the drug companies that create and manufacture drugs to fight disease, relieve pain, treat injuries, and so on. Lots of chemists work in this industry. Chemists work in the food industry, enriching and preserving the things we eat. Agriculture depends on chemistry. All those things in the bathroom were developed by chemists: soaps and detergents, cleansers, stain removers, shampoo, hair color, mouthwash, deodorant, toothpaste. Chemists are at work in many industries and government agencies.

BB: Does everybody who studies chemistry become a chemist?

AS: People may use their understanding of chemistry to launch into other interesting professions. One chemist I know is now a multimedia designer. His chemistry training prepared his mind for the demanding work of creating computer programs that help students learn about science subjects in interesting and fun ways. Others might move into university administration, law enforcement, government work, medicine, or business. And many students who start in chemistry move on to other fields of science and engineering because chemistry is recognized as the basic science. Knowledge of matter and its fundamental behaviors is a good place to start with any career in science.

BB: What tools and instruments do you use when you are doing your chemistry work?

AS: We use lots of different instruments to help us find out what things are made out of and how they are put together. As it turns out, some of our most important tools use light to give us information. The way different wavelengths of light are absorbed, reflected, or changed by substances tells us a lot about their structure.

Separation techniques are important, too. You undoubtedly used evaporation as a way to separate a solvent from a solute in your study of mixtures and solutions. You may have used chromatography to separate the pigments in inks. We do the same kinds of things when we are confronted with complex mixtures of substances. This part of chemistry is called analysis: finding and identifying all the parts in mixtures.

BB: Have you invented or discovered anything?

AS: My specialty is materials. I was investigating superconductors. Superconductors conduct electricity without resistance. But now I have turned my attention to trying to develop a new kind of refrigerator. Most refrigerators today use a gas called freon. But

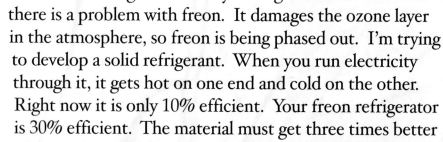

there is a problem with freon. It damages the ozone layer in the atmosphere, so freon is being phased out. I'm trying to develop a solid refrigerant. When you run electricity through it, it gets hot on one end and cold on the other. Right now it is only 10% efficient. Your freon refrigerator is 30% efficient. The material must get three times better to be useful on a broad scale. This is what I am trying to discover in my lab. But breakthroughs don't come easily. Discovery is hard work.

BB: What are the most interesting things you get to do?

AS: Teaching [is one]. My refrigeration research with graduate students is a kind of high-level teaching. I also teach basic chemistry for undergraduates, and I'm developing new ways to teach chemistry at the high school level. Another interesting part of my work is sharing ideas with other chemists all over the world. I have friends and colleagues in many countries as a result of my work in chemistry.

BB: Is there anything else you would like to say to fifth graders about chemistry?

AS: There are lots of opportunities in chemistry and in science generally. Whatever your interests are, knowledge of science can be part of your plans. I'd like to remind girls particularly not to be intimidated by science. In science, you have the opportunity to find things out that might help to solve problems, like my work in refrigeration, or disease control, food production, [or] lots of other things. It's a good feeling to contribute to the knowledge of the world.

Summary: Elements

Before 1869 scientists organized the **elements** by placing them in order by weight. In 1869 Dmitry Ivanovich Mendeleyev organized the 60 known elements in a new way. He put the elements in short rows one over the other. This put elements with similar **chemical properties** in columns. It was called the **periodic table of the elements.**

Mendeleyev found that this new system wasn't exactly right. He had to leave gaps in the layout to get elements in the right property columns. Mendeleyev predicted that undiscovered elements went in the gaps. He could predict their properties and what other elements they would react with. Using Mendeleyev's periodic table, scientists filled in the missing elements. They found all 90 over the next 40 years.

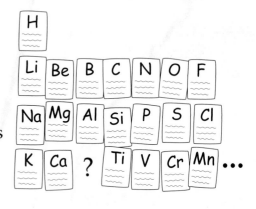

Early in the 1900s, scientists figured out that atoms are made of tiny particles called protons, neutrons, and electrons. Understanding the structure of the atom made it possible for scientists to develop the modern periodic table.

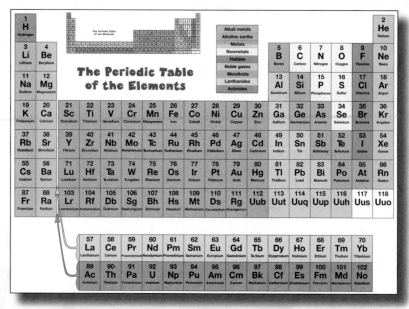

The periodic table provides interesting information. Sixty-five of the elements are **metals.** All of the elements shaded orange, blue, lavender, and yellow green are metals. Metals can be combined to make **alloys,** such as steel and brass. Thousands of alloys can be made from the 65 metallic elements.

All of the metals share several properties. They all have shiny luster and can be hammered and bent into new shapes without breaking. They also conduct heat and electricity well.

Most of the metals, however, are rare. Iron and magnesium are the exceptions. Iron is the most abundant element on Earth, and magnesium is the third most abundant. Iron, magnesium, and four other elements make up more than 98% of Earth.

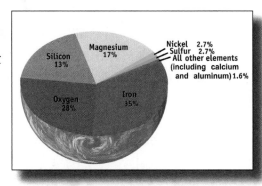

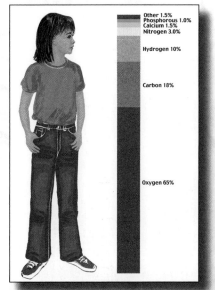

You are also made of elements. More than 98% of your body is composed of just six elements, too. But the six elements are different. You are made mostly of oxygen, carbon, and hydrogen. There is very little metal in your body. Calcium for strong bones is the most abundant metal.

The structure of the atom was figured out in the early 1900s. That gave scientists ideas about how atoms go together to form molecules. But because atoms are so small, no one could see them. In the early 1980s a new instrument, the **scanning tunneling microscope,** made it possible to see atoms. Scientists were able to confirm that atoms and molecules often occur in **well-ordered arrays.**

The most important advance in our understanding of the nature of matter was the discovery of the atom. After years of searching, scientists determined that there are 90 different kinds of atoms on Earth. Each atom defines an element. Elements are the basic substances from which all other substances are made. All the varied types of matter in the world are the result of the millions of different ways those 90 elements can go together.

Summary Questions

Now is a good time to review what you have recorded in your science notebook. Think about the investigations you have conducted with elements.

1. What is an atom?

2. What is an element?

3. Explain why there are so many different substances in the world.

4. What properties do all metals have in common?

5. What is the periodic table of the elements?

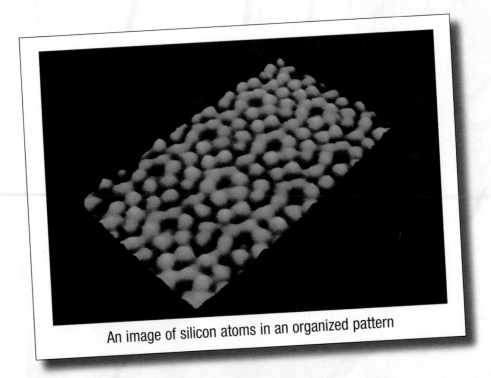

An image of silicon atoms in an organized pattern

California Science Standards

PS1c. Students know metals have properties in common, such as high electrical and thermal conductivity. Some metals, such as aluminum (Al), iron (Fe), nickel (Ni), copper (Cu), silver (Ag), and gold (Au), are pure elements; others, such as steel and brass, are composed of a combination of elemental metals.

PS1d. Students know that each element is made of one kind of atom and that the elements are organized in the periodic table by their chemical properties.

PS1e. Students know scientists have developed instruments that can create discrete images of atoms and molecules that show that the atoms and molecules often occur in well-ordered arrays.

PS1h. Students know living organisms and most materials are composed of just a few elements.

Vocabulary

element

chemical property

periodic table of the elements

metal

alloy

scanning tunneling microscope

well-ordered array

Learning More about Mixtures and Solutions

Mixtures and Solutions

Invent a Gorp Recipe

Invent a recipe for gorp (any mixture of nuts, dried fruits, and other goodies). List ingredients and amounts of each. Then share recipes with other students.

Find Out If It Dissolves

Try to make more solutions using water and the following:
- flour
- baking soda
- alum
- cooking oil
- rubbing alcohol

Research Diatomaceous Earth

Find out more about the origin of diatomaceous earth. Research its uses.

Research Sodium Chloride

Table salt is an important part of our lives. Research how salt gets to the table. Another research topic to consider is why some people are on low-salt diets.

Find Citric Acid

Many of the foods we eat and drink contain citric acid. It gives foods that tart taste. Read product labels and make a list of those that contain citric acid.

Make Saturated Solutions with Other Substances

Find out how much of common household materials it takes to saturate 50 milliliters of water. Try baking soda, alum, and sugar.

Change the Temperature

Collect and analyze data about the effect of temperature on the amount of solid material that will dissolve in a given amount of water. Repeat a few saturation experiments using hot water and ice water. Compare results.

Reactions

Apply the Reaction

Imagine a new product that you might invent as a result of one of the reactions in this investigation. What might that product be, how would it be used, and how would you sell it? Write descriptions and make illustrations.

Investigate Baking Powder and Baking Soda

Baking powder is different from baking soda, but both are used in cooking. Find out how they are the same and how they are different. The reaction of baking powder in water might suggest a difference and might be a clue to the ingredients in baking powder.

Physical Sciences Glossary

Alloy   A mixture of two or more metals.

Atom   The smallest particle of an element.

Atomic number   The number of protons in the nucleus of an atom.

Bends   A condition that causes pain in deep-sea divers' arms and legs after returning to the surface.

Caisson   A large box with no bottom. These boxes were used to provide environments for workers under water.

Carbohydrate   A group of carbon-based nutrients, such as sugars and starches.

Carbon-14 dating   A process used to find the age of carbon-based matter.

Carbon dioxide gas   A compound made from carbon and oxygen (CO_2).

Chemical equation   A model of a chemical reaction showing reactants and products.

Chemical formula   A code that tells how many and what kinds of atoms are in a substance.

Chemical property   A characteristic that describes how a substance is changed when it reacts with other substances.

Chemical reaction   The process in which two or more substances combine to make one or more new substances that have different properties than the original ones.

Compound   A substance made of two or more different kinds of atoms. Carbon dioxide (CO_2), sugar ($C_6H_{12}O_6$), and water (H_2O) are compounds. Oxygen (O_2) and hydrogen (H_2) are not compounds.

Crust   Earth's hard outer layer of solid rock.

Crystal   A natural form of a substance. Crystal shape is also a physical property that helps to identify a substance.

Cyclotron   An instrument used to create new elements.

Decompression   The change from higher pressure to lower pressure.

Diatomaceous earth   The skeletal remains of diatoms.

Dissolve   The process of a material becoming incorporated uniformly into another.

Electron   A subatomic particle with a negative charge.

Element   A fundamental substance that cannot be broken down by simple chemical and physical processes.

Evaporation   The change of state from a liquid to a gas.

Gas   Matter that is shapeless and expands to fill any closed container it is placed in.

Gaseous   Existing in the state of a gas (not a solid or liquid).

Global warming   Increase of average temperature worldwide.

Greenhouse gas   A gas, such as carbon dioxide, that contributes to global warming.

Insoluble   Not capable of being dissolved. Sand is insoluble in water.

Lipid   A group of nutrients that includes oils and fats.

Liquid   Matter that flows and takes the shape of the container it is in.

Mantle   The largest part of planet Earth which is found between Earth's core and crust.

Mass   A quantity of matter.

Matter   Anything that has mass and takes up space.

Metal   Elements that may be shiny, stretch and bend, but don't break, and conduct heat and electricity well.

Mixture   Two or more substances together.

Molecule   Particles made of two or more atoms that are held together with bonds. Carbon dioxide (CO_2), sugar ($C_6H_{12}O_6$), water (H_2O), oxygen (O_2), and hydrogen (H_2) are examples of molecules.

Neutron   A subatomic particle with no charge.

Nitrogen   A colorless, odorless, gaseous element that makes up about 78% of Earth's atmosphere.

Noble gas   A gas that does not react with other elements.

Nucleus   The center of an atom.

Octane   An eight-carbon molecule. Octane is one of the main ingredients in gasoline.

Ore   A rock or mineral that contains a valuable substance.

Oxidize   When oxygen reacts with a substance to make a new substance.

Particle   A very small piece or part.

Periodic table of the elements   A way to organize the elements based on atomic number.

Physical property   A characteristic that describes a substance, such as size, shape, and texture.

Potash   An impure form of potassium carbonate.

Predict   To make an accurate estimation of a future event based on knowledge.

Product   The substance(s) produced in a chemical reaction.

Protein   A group of nitrogen-containing substances produced by organisms.

Proton   A subatomic particle that has a positive charge.

Radiation   Energy sent out into space by an energy source.

Radioactivity   The radiation given off by the elements.

Reactant   The starting substance(s) in a chemical reaction.

Room temperature How hot or cold it is in an indoor space like a classroom or a house. Often room temperature is around 21°C (70°F).

Salt The product that forms when metals react with acid.

Saturated When the solvent cannot dissolve any more solute.

Scanning tunneling microscope (STM) An instrument that can create images of arrays of atoms.

Solid Matter that has a definite shape.

Solubility The ability of one substance to spread out uniformly throughout another substance.

Soluble Capable of being dissolved. Table salt is soluble in water.

Solute A substance that dissolves in a solvent to form a solution.

Solution A mixture formed when one or more substances dissolve in another.

Solvent A substance in which a solute dissolves to form a solution.

Supersaturated solution A solution that contains more solute than it normally would at a given temperature.

Transparent Clear. Describes something through which you can see an image clearly.

Voltaic pile Another name for an electric battery.

Volume Three-dimensional space.

Well-ordered array A repeating pattern.

Life Sciences

Living Systems

Life Sciences
Table of Contents
Living Systems

Living Cells

An amoeba is a living, single-celled organism (magnified 80 times).

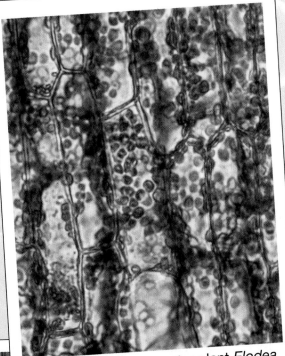

Cells in a leaf of the water plant *Elodea* (magnified 400 times)

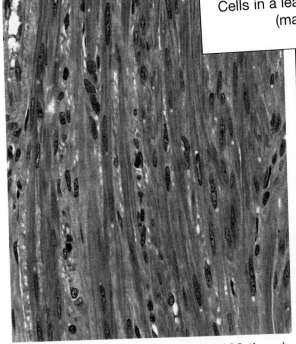

Human muscle cells (magnified 100 times)

LS2a. Students know many multicellular organisms have specialized structures to support the transport of materials.

LS2b. Students know how blood circulates through the heart chambers, lungs, and body and how carbon dioxide (CO_2) and oxygen (O_2) are exchanged in the lungs and tissues.

Circulatory System

The basic unit of life is the **cell.** All organisms are made of living cells. The simplest organisms, such as the amoeba, are just one cell.

All living cells have something in common. They all have a **membrane** on the outside. All cells are filled with a liquid called **cytoplasm,** which is mostly water. And all cells need four resources in order to stay alive. They are **water,** food, gases, and **waste disposal.**

How Do Cells Get Resources?

Single-celled organisms live in water. The food and gases they need to survive are in the water. The environment brings water, food, and gases to the cells all the time. The cell releases waste products into the water. The environment provides all the resources that single-celled organisms need.

A human is a **multicellular organism.** A human is made of trillions of cells. Humans don't live in water, and most of the cells are deep inside the body.

A living amoeba

Muscles are made of millions of cells. Every cell in a human muscle is alive. That means every cell is getting the resources it needs to survive. How do these muscle cells get the water, food, gases, and waste removal they need to survive?

Multicellular organisms have **specialized structures** to **transport** resources to cells. In humans, blood, which is mostly water, is pumped through blood vessels to all the cells. The blood carries food and gases to the cells, and carries away wastes.

Resource Delivery

Blood flows through blood vessels to every cell in the body. The blood is kept flowing with a pump called the **heart.** The heart is a four-chambered organ made of powerful muscles. The muscles contract to pump the blood about once every second. You can feel the beat of your pumping heart when you put your hand on your chest. The heart muscle works all the time. It pumps day and night, year after year. Every year your heart beats more than 30 million times!

Blood flows away from the heart in blood vessels called **arteries.** Blood flows back to the heart in vessels called **veins.** The smallest blood vessels, the ones that serve the cells, are called **capillaries.** The system of blood vessels and the heart is called the **circulatory system.** It **circulates** blood to every cell in your body.

The two most important resources transported to cells are **oxygen** (a gas) and **sugar** (food). The most important waste product removed from cells is **carbon dioxide** (a gas). Oxygen comes from the air we breathe, and sugar comes from the food we eat. In order to get fresh oxygen, dispose of carbon dioxide, and get new sugar for cells, the circulatory system has to connect with the **lungs** and **intestines.**

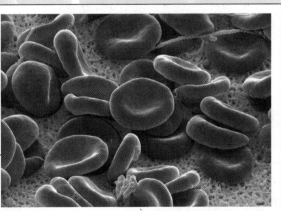
Red blood cells (magnified 2,520 times)

To learn how the circulatory system works, let's take an imaginary trip through it. We will ride on a red blood cell. Red blood cells carry oxygen to the cells and carbon dioxide away from the cells. You have about 25 trillion red blood cells in your body. They live only about 4 months, so they are being replaced at the amazing rate of about 3 million per second.

The Right Side of the Heart

It takes about a minute for a red blood cell to travel once through the circulatory system. Blood returning from the body cells goes to the right side of the heart. The returning red blood cells are carrying carbon dioxide waste. The returning blood enters the upper chamber on the right side of the heart called the **right atrium.** When the heart beats, the right atrium gets squeezed. It pushes blood down into the **right ventricle.**

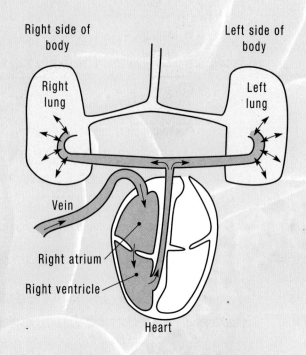

The next time the heart beats, it pushes blood out of the right ventricle to the lungs. The blood flows through tiny capillaries that are touching the air sacs in the lungs. The red blood cells release carbon dioxide. The carbon dioxide enters the air in the lungs and is exhaled. Then the red blood cells take oxygen from the air you breathe in.

The Left Side of the Heart

The oxygen-rich red blood cells go back to the left side of the heart. Blood from the lungs flows into the **left atrium.** The next time the heart beats, it squeezes blood into the powerful **left ventricle.** When the left ventricle contracts, it pumps blood through arteries to the body. The red blood cells transport oxygen and pick up waste carbon dioxide. Then the cycle starts over again.

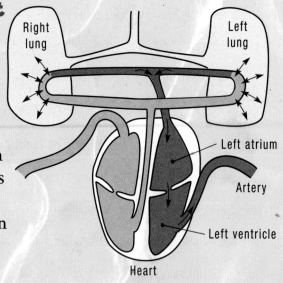

Gas Exchange in the Lungs and Cells

The human body is made of many different kinds of cells. There are nerve cells, muscle cells, bone cells, liver cells, lung cells, skin cells, and so on. A group of cells of the same kind, working together to perform a function, is called a **tissue.** Muscle tissue contracts to produce movement. Bone tissue gives our bodies structure. Nerve tissue sends electric messages. Each tissue is made of its own kinds of cells. But the cells in all tissues need the same basic resources.

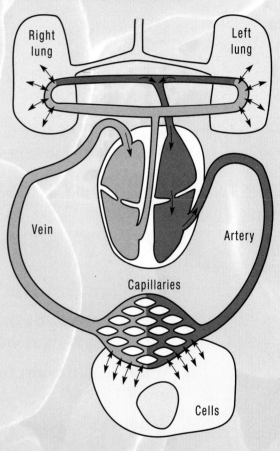

Cells break down sugar to get **energy.** Cells need oxygen (O_2) to do the job. One of the by-products of the sugar breakdown is the waste gas carbon dioxide (CO_2). If cells don't get O_2, they will die. If cells don't get rid of the CO_2, they will die.

Blood flows to the body tissues through arteries. The blood flows through smaller and smaller arteries, ending in networks of capillaries. Capillaries are only 1/100 of a millimeter in diameter. That's just a little bit larger than a red blood cell. Capillaries are so small that red blood cells often have to go single file to get through.

The capillaries touch every cell in the body. Gas exchange takes place while the red blood cell is sliding past a cell. Here only the thin wall of the capillary is between them. Oxygen passes into the cells, and carbon dioxide passes out. The red blood cell then transports the carbon dioxide to the lungs for disposal.

Red blood cells in capillaries
(magnified 100 times)

89

The **respiratory system** has two main parts. They are the lungs and the system of tubes that connect the lungs with the outside air. The respiratory system brings oxygen to the red blood cells and gets rid of carbon dioxide.

The circulatory system has three main parts. They are the blood, the blood vessels through which the blood flows, and the heart that pumps the blood. The blood transports resources to the cells.

So far we have focused on the work done by the red blood cells in the blood. Red blood cells carry gases. They carry the essential gas oxygen to the cells and carry the waste gas carbon dioxide away from the cells.

The circulatory system has other functions, too. We will find out about these later when we learn about the digestive and excretory systems.

Review Questions

1. **What are the basic needs of all living cells?**

2. **How do the cells in multicellular organisms get the resources they need to stay alive?**

3. **What is the main function of the left side of the human heart?**

4. **What is the main function of the right side of the human heart?**

5. **What is the function of the red blood cells?**

6. **What are the main kinds of blood vessels and what functions do they perform?**

7. **Describe what happens when blood flows through the lungs.**

8. **Describe what happens when blood in capillaries flows past cells.**

LS2a. Students know many multicellular organisms have specialized structures to support the transport of materials.

LS2c. Students know the sequential steps of digestion and the roles of teeth and the mouth, esophagus, stomach, small intestine, large intestine, and colon in the function of the digestive system.

LS2d. Students know the role of the kidney in removing cellular waste from blood and converting it into urine, which is stored in the bladder.

The Disassembly Line

It happens all the time. You get hungry and you have something to eat. After school some crackers and cheese and a glass of fruit juice might be just the thing. Then in the evening, you eat again. In the morning you start all over again with breakfast, lunch, and so on for the rest of your life. Why do you always have to eat?

You eat to feed the trillions of living cells that are your body. Every cell has work to do. Muscle cells contract to make muscles work. Nerve cells send electric messages. Skin cells divide to make new skin cells. All the different things cells do require energy and raw materials for building. Cells get energy and raw materials from three groups of **nutrients.** These groups are **carbohydrates, fats,** and **proteins.** The process of breaking human food into nutrients for cells is called **digestion.**

The Digestive System

Turning cheese, crackers, and juice into nutrients for cells starts in your **mouth. Teeth** cut, mash, and grind large pieces of food into small particles. **Saliva** mixes with the food to get it wet and to start the chemical breakdown of the food. When the food is thoroughly chewed and moistened, it is swallowed. A

wad of food, called a **bolus,** leaves the mouth and starts
down the **esophagus** toward the **stomach.** Muscles
along the length of the esophagus contract to push the
bolus along. Your stomach is not just a place where
a meal is stored. Things get rough down there.
Digestive juices, including acid, are added to
the food. Muscles in the stomach squeeze
and mash the food. The food changes
into a thick, runny liquid.

The food moves into the **small
intestine,** which can be 6 meters
(20 feet) long. More digestive
juices are added. This is where
food changes into nutrients that
cells can use. The most important
nutrient is sugar.

The small intestine is lined with
millions of capillaries. Sugar and
other nutrients pass through the
sides of the intestine into the
capillaries. The nutrient-rich
blood then flows throughout
your body, providing food
for cells.

The undigested
leftovers of the food leave
the small intestine and
enter the **large intestine**
and **colon.** By this time,
most of the nutrients have
been taken out. Bacteria
living in the colon break down
the remaining usable food.
Water is taken out of the food
mass. The remaining material
is composed of fiber, indigestible material, and dead bacteria.
This is called feces. The feces moves into the rectum. Here the
waste is held until it can be eliminated through the anus.

Mouth

Esophagus

Right
lung

Left
lung

Heart

Stomach

Cells

Small intestine

Colon

Large intestine

Rectum

Anus

92

Cleaning the Blood

The breakdown of food continues in the cells. After sugars, proteins, and fats have been disassembled, all that is left are waste chemicals. These waste chemicals, along with bits of dead cells, salts, and acids, end up in the blood flow. If these waste materials were allowed to build up, the environment would soon be unfit to support living cells. But you have two very good blood cleaners. They are your **kidneys.**

Kidneys are located beside your backbone just below your ribs. Twenty percent of the blood leaving the left ventricle of your heart goes directly to your kidneys. Every day all of your blood is cleaned 20 to 25 times by your kidneys.

Kidneys act like filters, separating the **cellular wastes** from the blood. The waste materials, including salts and nitrogen compounds, are removed from the blood and converted to **urine.** The urine flows through a tube into your **bladder** for storage.

The kidneys and bladder are part of the **excretory system.**

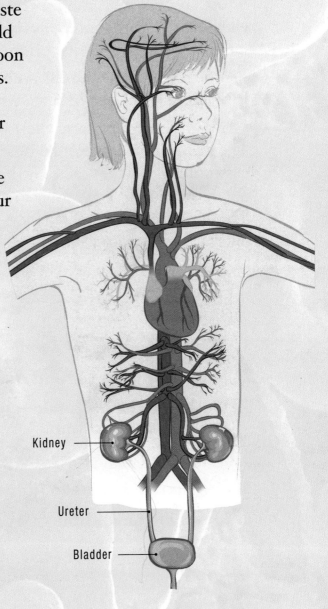

Kidney

Ureter

Bladder

The Big Picture

Every cell in multicellular organisms needs nutrients. Nutrients are transported to the cells by blood. Food is one source of those nutrients.

Most of the foods we eat cannot be used by cells. Food, like bread, cheese, meat, and fruit, must be broken down into simple chemicals. The **digestive system** breaks complex food sources into simple chemicals that cells can use. Those simple chemicals then enter the bloodstream. Once in the blood, nutrients can travel to all the cells.

Blood is also the place where cellular waste is "dumped." The waste products must be cleaned up to keep a healthy environment for the cells. The kidneys filter the waste products out of the blood. The waste then leaves the body in the urine. The digestive system and kidneys work together to provide nutrients and remove waste.

Review Questions

1. **Why do people eat food?**
2. **What happens to food in the digestive system?**
3. **Describe the path taken by food as it passes through the digestive system.**
4. **How does digested food get to cells?**
5. **Why do people need kidneys?**
6. **Describe how kidneys work.**

Summary: Living Cells

ife is everywhere on Earth. Living organisms can be as big as the blue whales that live in the ocean off the California coast. Living organisms can be as small as the bacteria living in your intestines. As different as living organisms are from one another, they all share one thing. All organisms are made of **cells.**

Most of the organisms on Earth are single-celled organisms. That means they are made of only one cell. But Earth also has millions of kinds of **multicellular organisms** that are made of many cells. It doesn't matter whether the cell is living alone or with many others. All cells need resources to stay alive. Every living cell needs **water,** food, gases, and **waste disposal.**

Single-celled organisms live in water. They get water, food, gases, and waste disposal directly from their environment. But multicellular organisms don't all live in water, and many cells are not in contact with water. How do cells in multicellular organisms get the resources they need to survive?

Multicellular organisms have systems to **transport** water, food, and gases to the cells, and to transport wastes away from the cells. Those systems are the respiratory system, circulatory system, digestive system, and excretory system.

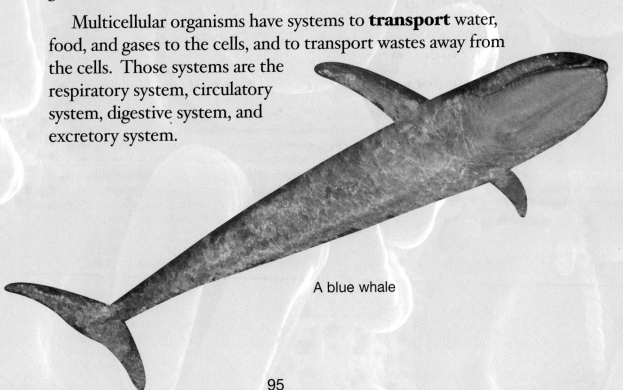

A blue whale

95

Respiratory System

Cells need **oxygen.** When you breathe in, oxygen from the air enters your **lungs.** Millions of air sacs in your lungs are surrounded by **capillaries.** The oxygen passes through the walls of the air sacs into the capillaries. Red blood cells pick up the oxygen.

Red blood cells also release the waste gas **carbon dioxide** into the lung sacs. When you breathe out, carbon dioxide goes into the atmosphere. Breathing transports oxygen to the blood and carries carbon dioxide away from the blood.

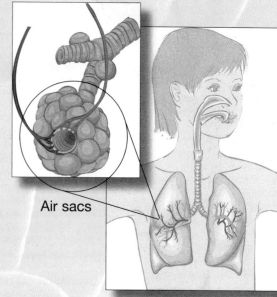

Air sacs

Human respiratory system

Circulatory System

Your **heart** pumps blood through the **circulatory system** to bring resources to every cell. Oxygen-rich blood flows from your lungs to the left side of your heart. The left side of your heart pumps blood out to all parts of your body in **arteries.** The arteries branch until the blood flows into the tiny capillaries. The capillaries are in contact with your cells. Oxygen, water, and food are transferred to the cells, and carbon dioxide is carried away. Blood flows back to the right side of the heart in **veins.** The right side of your heart pumps blood to your lungs. And the cycle continues over and over.

Human circulatory system

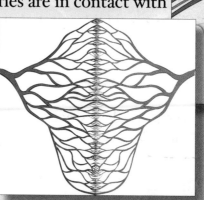

Capillary network

Digestive System

Cells do a lot of work. Work calls for **energy.** Cells get energy from food. But the food you eat is not the food needed by cells. The food you eat changes into cell nutrients in the **digestive system.**

Digestion starts in your **mouth.** When you chew a handful of nuts and dry fruit, the food is crushed by your **teeth** and moistened by saliva. The snack then passes into your **stomach** through the **esophagus.** Digestive juices turn the food into a thick liquid, which passes into the **small intestine.** During its long trip through the small intestine, the food breaks down into **sugars** and other simple nutrients. The nutrients pass through the intestine walls into the blood for transport to the cells. The unused parts of the food you eat pass into the **large intestine** and **colon.** Here water is removed. The waste becomes solid, ready for elimination.

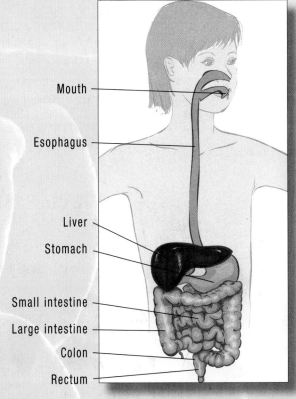

Mouth

Esophagus

Liver

Stomach

Small intestine

Large intestine

Colon

Rectum

Human digestive system

Excretory System

Cells produce waste. The waste chemicals are "dumped" into the bloodstream. **Cellular wastes** are removed by your **kidneys.** Kidneys act like filters. Waste chemicals are filtered out and converted to **urine.** The urine collects in the **bladder.** The wastes leave the body during urination.

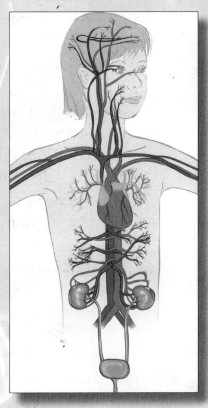

Human excretory system

Summary Questions

Now is a good time to review what you have recorded in your science notebook. Think about the four specialized systems that provide life support for cells in multicellular organisms.

1. What support does the digestive system provide for cells?

2. What support does the respiratory system provide for cells?

3. What support does the circulatory system provide for cells?

4. What support does the kidney provide for cells?

Vocabulary

cell
multicellular organism
water
waste disposal
transport
respiratory system
oxygen
lung
capillary
carbon dioxide
heart
circulatory system
artery
vein
energy
digestive system
digestion
mouth and teeth
stomach
esophagus
small intestine
sugar
large intestine
colon
excretory system
cellular waste
kidney
urine
bladder

California Science Standards

LS2a. Students know many multicellular organisms have specialized structures to support the transport of materials.

LS2b. Students know how blood circulates through the heart chambers, lungs, and body and how carbon dioxide (CO_2) and oxygen (O_2) are exchanged in the lungs and tissues.

LS2c. Students know the sequential steps of digestion and the roles of teeth and the mouth, esophagus, stomach, small intestine, large intestine, and colon in the function of the digestive system.

LS2d. Students know the role of the kidney in removing cellular waste from blood and converting it into urine, which is stored in the bladder.

Extensions

Math Problem of the Week

Jan and Rosa were playing a game with two dice. It seemed like the number 7 came up all the time. They wondered why.

Does 7 come up more often than the other numbers? Hint: A grid might help you answer this question.

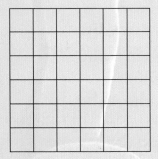

Home/School Connection

Listen to your body's transport systems. They make sounds! Use a stethoscope to listen, if you have one. You can make a simple listening device with two small plastic cups and a short piece of plastic tubing.

Make a small hole in the bottom of both cups with a nail. Force the tubing into the holes. It should fit very tightly.

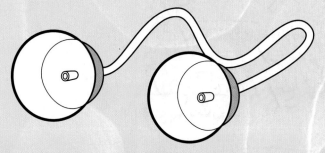

Put the mouth of one cup over the thing you want to hear. Put the other cup over your ear. Listen to your heart, lungs, stomach, intestines, your throat swallowing, and your teeth chewing.

What are those other sounds? Find out what causes hiccups, burps, stomach growls, and sneezes.

INVESTIGATION 2

LS2a. Students know many multicellular organisms have specialized structures to support the transport of materials.

LS2e. Students know how sugar, water, and minerals are transported in a vascular plant.

Vascular Plants

General Sherman is the name of the biggest organism in the world. It stands over 85 meters tall (280 feet) and is 11 meters (36 feet) wide at the base. General Sherman is a giant sequoia redwood tree living in Sequoia National Park in California.

Like all living organisms, General Sherman is made of living cells. Every cell needs water, nutrients, gases, and waste removal. How do all of General Sherman's billions of cells get the resources they need to survive?

General Sherman is a **vascular plant.** Other vascular plants include wildflowers, sagebrush, cacti, orange trees, lettuce, strawberries, wheat, and celery. All vascular plants have a system of tubes running through them. These specialized structures transport nutrients to all the cells.

General Sherman, the world's largest living organism

Xylem

Vascular plants have roots that reach deep into the soil. The roots take up water from the soil. The water enters long, hollow tubes called **xylem.** The xylem tubes start as long cells that are connected end to end. When the tubes are complete, the cells die. The resulting tubes are used to transport water and minerals to the cells at the very top of General Sherman and to all the other living cells as well.

If you cut across the trunk of a tree, you can see the ends of the xylem tubes. New xylem cells grow all the time. The old xylem tubes form the main trunk of the tree. We call the old xylem cells wood.

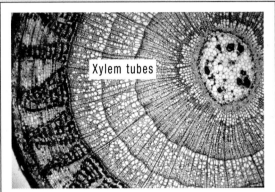

Xylem tubes carry water and minerals from the roots to the cells in the plant.

Phloem

The green leaves of plants produce sugar. The sugar is the food used by all the cells in the plant. Some cells, like root cells and flower cells, do not make sugar. They need to get sugar from the cells that make it.

Vascular plants have a second kind of tube called **phloem.** Phloem tubes transport a sugar-rich liquid called **sap.** The phloem delivers sugar to every living cell that cannot make its own sugar.

Celery cross section

Many vascular plants have specialized structures called **vascular bundles.** A vascular bundle includes a bunch of xylem tubes and phloem tubes. The celery stalk you investigated has vascular bundles. With a microscope, you can see the xylem and phloem.

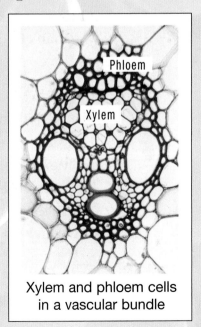

Xylem and phloem cells in a vascular bundle

Transporting Nutrients to the Leaves

The xylem and phloem in vascular plants are a little like the arteries and veins in humans. Take a close look at the illustration below. You can see how the xylem transports water and **minerals** to the cells in a vascular plant.

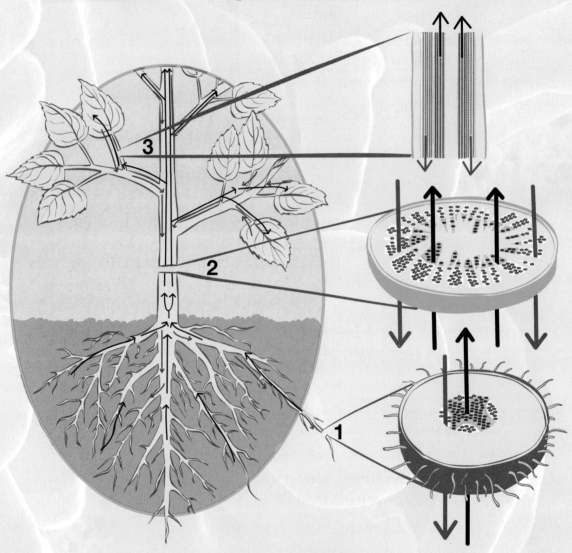

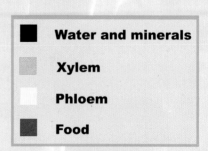

Water enters the roots underground. At number 1, a short section of root was cut. The section is shown enlarged. The tissue illustrated in pink is the xylem. Water and minerals dissolved in the water flow up the root toward the stem. The black arrow shows the direction that water and minerals move through the xylem tubes.

⬛	**Water and minerals**
▨	**Xylem**
⬜	**Phloem**
▦	**Food**

At number 2, a section of stem was cut. The section has been enlarged. The xylem from all the roots passes through the stem. Often a group of xylem cells is found close to a group of phloem cells. They form a vascular bundle. You can see a lot of vascular bundles around the outside of the stem.

At number 3, a section of leaf stem was cut. The section was cut again from top to bottom. In the enlarged view you can see the xylem carrying nutrients and water to the cells in the leaves.

The xylem tubes end in spaces between the cells in the leaves. Minerals and some of the water are taken in by the cells. The rest of the water evaporates through tiny holes in the leaves.

Transporting Sugar to the Cells

Plants make sugar from carbon dioxide and water when the Sun shines. The sugar is made in green plant cells. Cells use the sugar for energy. Extra sugar passes out of the cells into the tiny phloem tubes. The sugar mixes with water to make a sweet liquid called sap. The sap flows through the phloem to all the cells that are not green. Cells that are not green can't make their own sugar.

Look at the vascular-plant illustration again. This time follow the red arrows. From the leaf, the sugar flows through the tiny leaf stem (number 3) into the branches. The phloem in all the branches comes together in the main stem (number 2). Finally the phloem branches out into all the roots, delivering sugar to all the cells in even the tiniest root (number 1). Every cell receives energy-rich sugar so it can stay alive and do its job.

Comparing Plants and Animals

Multicellular animals and vascular plants have specialized structures to transport nutrients. In both plants and animals, nutrients flow through systems of vessels. But the systems in animals are different from the systems in plants. Animals have one system of vessels. Blood flows from the heart to the cells in arteries. Nutrients transfer to the cells in the capillaries. Then the blood returns to the heart in veins. Blood goes around and around, transporting everything cells need.

Plants have two systems of vessels that are not connected. Water flows from the roots through xylem tubes to all the cells. The water carries minerals as it goes. Extra water then evaporates into the air. Water passes *through* the plant. It does not circulate like the blood in animals.

Water and sugar come out of cells and flow to all the other cells in phloem tubes. The phloem carries only food for cells.

Plants have two "one-way" systems. One system transports water and minerals up, and the other system transports sugar down. Animals have one system that goes around and around.

Review Questions

1. **What specialized structures in vascular plants transport sugar?**

2. **What specialized structures in vascular plants transport water and minerals?**

3. **In what ways are the transport systems the same for plants and animals?**

4. **In what ways are the transport systems different for plants and animals?**

Classification

Most vascular plants have leaves. The leaves on one kind of plant are different from the leaves on other kinds of plants. Scientists can use leaves to identify plants. But with so many different kinds of plants in the world, how do scientists use leaves to identify plants? The answer is classification systems.

Leaves have properties that can be used to organize them into groups, or classes. In class you used the pattern of veins in the leaves to organize your leaf collection. You organized the leaves into three classes, **palmate, pinnate,** and **parallel.**

Palmate

Pinnate

Parallel

Other properties can be used to **classify** leaves, too. Leaves have shape. Some are long and pointed. Others are round. Leaves can even be square, triangle, or heart shaped. You can classify leaves by the shape of the **blade.**

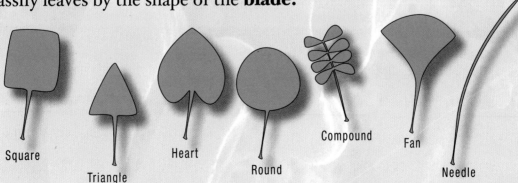

Spear

Square

Triangle

Heart

Round

Compound

Fan

Needle

The edges of leaves, called **margins,** are different from one another. Margins can be smooth, saw-toothed, lobed, or fuzzy. You can classify leaves by their margins.

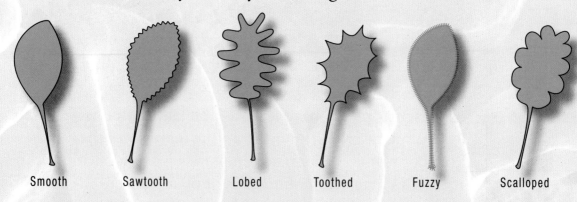

Smooth   Sawtooth   Lobed   Toothed   Fuzzy   Scalloped

Leaves are not the only things that can be classified. Whole plants can be classified. They can be organized into grasses, clovers, cacti, sagebrushes, palm trees, and so on. Rocks can be classified by the minerals they contain or by the manner in which they form. A collection of rocks can be divided into a set that contains mica, another set that contains calcite, a third set that contains quartz, and so on. The same collection of rocks can be classified again into sets of igneous, sedimentary, and metamorphic rocks.

Classification is one of the ways scientists organize information about the natural world. By putting things together that have the same properties or behaviors, the complex world becomes a little easier to understand.

Review Questions

1. **What is classification?**

2. **What are three different ways you can classify leaves?**

3. **If you had a collection of insects, what ways might you classify them?**

Summary: Vascular Plants

Plants are living organisms. In order to stay alive, the cells in plants need a steady supply of water, **minerals,** and sugar.

Vascular plants are multicellular organisms. They have two specialized systems of tubes that transport water, minerals, and sugar to all the plant's cells.

One system of tubes is **xylem.** Xylem tubes start in the roots and end in the leaves. Water flows in the xylem to every cell in the plant. The water also carries dissolved minerals to the cells.

The other system of tubes is **phloem.** Phloem carries a mixture of water and sugar called **sap** to all the cells that need it. The phloem tubes start in the leaves and end in the roots.

Sap flows from the leaves to the roots through the phloem tubes.

Water and minerals flow through the plant from the roots to the leaves in xylem tubes.

Seeing Xylem and Phloem

Xylem tubes and phloem tubes are often found close together forming **vascular bundles.** When you put a celery stalk in red water, the red color stains the xylem tubes. This makes it easy to see the vascular bundles in the celery.

Another place that vascular bundles are easy to see is in the leaves. The veins are actually vascular bundles. Each major vein has a bunch of xylem tubes transporting water to the leaf cells. The vein also has a bunch of phloem tubes transporting sugar away from the leaf cells.

Xylem and phloem cells in a vascular bundle

Classifying Leaves

The pattern of leaf veins is different for each plant. The veins on an apple tree leaf are different from the veins on a maple leaf or a palm leaf. But all the leaves on one kind of plant have the same vein pattern. All apple tree leaves have a **pinnate** pattern. All maple leaves have a **palmate** pattern. All palm leaves have a **parallel** pattern. The pattern of leaf veins is one way to **classify** leaves.

Pinnate

Palmate

Parallel

Comparing Plants and Animals

Vascular plants and animals have systems for transporting nutrients to all their cells. Animals, like humans, have one circulatory system to serve all the needs of their cells. Vascular plants have two systems to serve the needs of their cells. The xylem system provides water and minerals. The phloem system provides sugar. Animals transport nutrients in one system that flows around and around. Plants transport nutrients in two systems that flow only one way.

Summary Questions

Now is a good time to review what you have recorded in your science notebook. Think about the two transport systems in vascular plants and how transport is similar and different in animals.

1. Describe how all the cells in a vascular plant get sugar.

2. Describe how all the cells in a vascular plant get water and minerals.

3. Why do its leaves turn pink when a celery stalk is placed in red water?

4. In what way are blood and sap the same?

California Science Standards

LS2a. Students know many multicellular organisms have specialized structures to support the transport of materials.

LS2e. Students know how sugar, water, and minerals are transported in a vascular plant.

I&E6a. Classify objects (e.g., rocks, plants, leaves) in accordance with appropriate criteria.

Vocabulary

mineral

vascular plant

xylem

phloem

sap

vascular bundle

pinnate

palmate

parallel

classify

Extensions

Math Problem of the Week

Roger put a stalk of celery with six leaves in 100 milliliters (ml) of water. Sixteen hours later, there was only 88 ml of water left in the cup.

Lucetta put a stalk of celery in 100 ml of water. Two days (48 hours) later, only 40 ml of water was left in the cup.

How many leaves were on Lucetta's celery stalk?

NOTE: The celery leaves averaged 4 square centimeters.

Home/School Connection

You know how celery takes up water. Will water pass through other plant stems and leaves? You can use colored water to find out. Get a few plants at the produce market to investigate. Try different kinds of cabbage and lettuce, green onions and leeks, asparagus, and other interesting things.

LS2f. Students know plants use carbon dioxide (CO_2) and energy from sunlight to build molecules of sugar and release oxygen.

Making Food

Paco and Eva learned that plants produce food. If that's true, they thought, then plants should increase in mass as they grow. But where would the mass come from? Paco and Eva decided to find out by doing an experiment.

Paco got a bag of beans, and Eva filled a big tray with sand. They set up their experiment like this.

1. Weigh exactly 500 grams of beans.

2. Plant them in exactly 10,000 grams of sand.

500 g

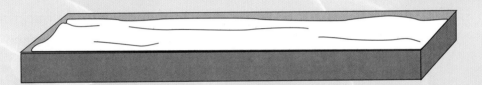

3. Put 1 gram of fertilizer in 10 liters of water and use it to water the beans every day.

4. After 3 weeks carefully dig up the bean plants and weigh them.

The two students ran their experiment. When the 3 weeks had passed, they dug up and weighed the bean plants. The mass of the plants was 565 grams.

565 g

Paco and Eva brought their results to class and presented their conclusions. They concluded that plants do make food. Their evidence was the increased mass of the beans.

Students in their class had questions for Paco and Eva.

• How do you know the increased mass was food produced by the beans? Maybe the beans just soaked up water.

• Where did the mass of food come from? The sand? The air?

Paco and Eva agreed that more information was needed to figure out where the increased mass came from. But how could they find out? They needed help.

Redesigning the Experiment

Paco and Eva visited Professor Welch at the college in their community. Professor Welch is a **botanist,** a scientist who studies plants. They talked about the questions that came up in class. Professor Welch had some suggestions for how to get more information.

Was the increase in mass the result of water soaking into the plants? Professor Welch said that the way to find out is to dry the plants after they have grown for 3 weeks. The dry mass of the beans after growing can then be compared to the dry mass of the beans before growing.

Did the increased mass come from the sand? Professor Welch suggested that again dry mass should answer the question. Weigh the mass of sand before and after the beans have grown. Compare the masses.

Did the increased mass come from the air? Professor Welch said this was a more complicated question because air is composed of several gases. Three of the gases, nitrogen, oxygen, and carbon dioxide, need to be tested. Professor Welch said he had environment chambers in his lab that could be used to test the effect of each of the gases.

Then Professor Welch said there was one more **variable** the students should test. Light.

Paco and Eva wrote down the variables they would consider in their new experiment.

Dry mass
Water
Nitrogen
Oxygen
Carbon dioxide
Light

After a lot of thinking, Paco and Eva had a plan. They would place six planters in six identical environment chambers. The chambers would allow them to control water, light, and air—oxygen (O_2), carbon dioxide (CO_2), and nitrogen (N_2). The table below summarizes the conditions in each chamber.

	Water	Light	O_2	CO_2	N_2
Experiment A	Yes	Yes	Yes	Yes	Yes
Experiment B	Yes	Yes	Yes	Yes	No
Experiment C	Yes	Yes	Yes	No	Yes
Experiment D	Yes	Yes	No	Yes	Yes
Experiment E	Yes	No	Yes	Yes	Yes
Experiment F	No	Yes	Yes	Yes	Yes

Note that experiment A provides the plants with water, light, oxygen, carbon dioxide, and nitrogen. Each of the other five experiments provides only four of the five variables. A different variable is missing in each chamber.

Experimental Results

After the plants spent 3 weeks in the experimental chambers, Paco and Eva carefully removed them from each tray of sand. They dried the beans and the sand completely, and weighed them. The masses of the plants and sand are recorded in the table below.

	Bean starting mass (g)	Bean ending mass (g)	Sand starting mass (g)	Sand ending mass (g)
Environment A	500	551	10,000	10,000
Environment B	500	552	10,000	10,000
Environment C	500	500	10,000	10,000
Environment D	500	549	10,000	10,000
Environment E	500	500	10,000	10,000
Environment F	500	500	10,000	10,000

Paco and Eva studied their data. They could see that beans grown for 3 weeks with water, light, oxygen, carbon dioxide, and nitrogen increased in mass. Those conditions were pretty much the same as in a garden where beans get light, water, and air. But it was the other experiments that provided more information.

After talking it over, Paco and Eva arrived at new conclusions. They were ready to present the additional information to their class and share their findings.

What conclusions about food production by plants do you think Paco and Eva shared with their class?

Review Questions

1. **Do plants produce food when they have no water?**

2. **Do plants produce food when they have no light?**

3. **Do plants produce food when they have no nitrogen?**

4. **Do plants produce food when they have no oxygen?**

5. **Do plants produce food when they have no carbon dioxide?**

6. **Do plants produce food from the sand they grow in?**

7. **What variables are essential for plants to produce food?**

8. **Where does the mass of the produced food come from?**

9. **Explain how Paco and Eva's data support your conclusion.**

LS2f. Students know plants use carbon dioxide (CO_2) and energy from sunlight to build molecules of sugar and release oxygen.

Photosynthesis

Plants produce their own food. The food is energy-rich sugar. The sugar is used by all plant cells. The cells use the energy in the sugar to do the things they do.

Plants use a process called **photosynthesis** to make sugar. The raw materials are water and carbon dioxide. The water and carbon dioxide combine with solar energy. Sugar and oxygen are the products.

Where Does Photosynthesis Happen?

Most plants are green. Or at least they have a lot of green leaves. Leaves look green because the leaf cells contain the molecule **chlorophyll.** Chlorophyll can absorb red and blue light. It reflects green light. That's why chlorophyll looks green.

The important part is that chlorophyll absorbs blue and red light. The energy from the absorbed blue and red light is then ready to be put into the sugar molecules during photosynthesis.

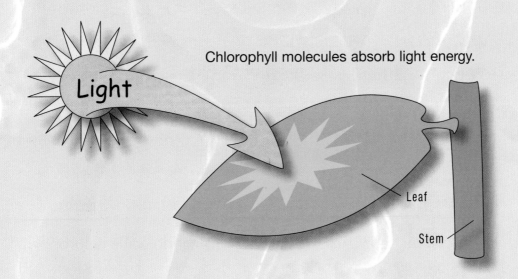

Chlorophyll molecules absorb light energy.

Light

Leaf

Stem

The green leaf cells make sugar out of two raw materials. They are carbon dioxide (CO_2) and water (H_2O). Carbon dioxide comes from the air. Water comes through xylem tubes from the roots. The carbon dioxide and water enter the green cells.

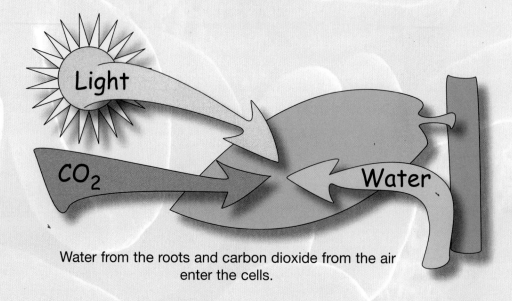

Water from the roots and carbon dioxide from the air enter the cells.

The carbon dioxide, water, and energy from the Sun combine to make sugar molecules in the plant's cells. Oxygen molecules are also produced. The oxygen is released into the air.

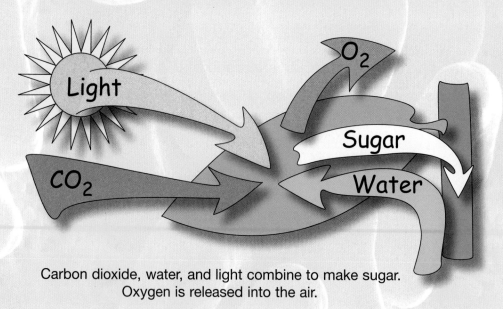

Carbon dioxide, water, and light combine to make sugar. Oxygen is released into the air.

So where is food produced? In the green parts of the plant. Every cell that contains the light-absorbing molecule chlorophyll is making sugar.

The Photosynthesis Equation

Sugar is in a class of substances called carbohydrates. Carbohydrates are always made of just three kinds of atoms, carbon, hydrogen, and oxygen. These three kinds of atoms can be connected with bonds in thousands of different ways. One way makes **glucose,** the sugar made in cells during photosynthesis. This is a model of a glucose molecule.

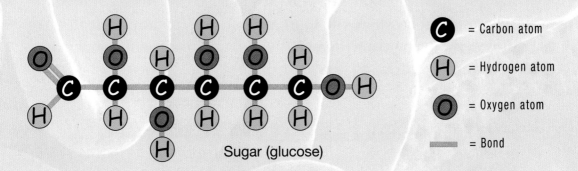

Sugar (glucose)

C = Carbon atom

H = Hydrogen atom

O = Oxygen atom

= Bond

The glucose molecule is built from carbon dioxide molecules and water molecules. Those molecules look like this.

Carbon dioxide

Water

It takes a lot of carbon dioxide and water molecules to make one sugar molecule. Here's what the equation looks like.

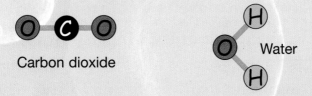

$$6\ CO_2 + 12\ H_2O + \text{Solar energy} \rightarrow C_6H_{12}O_6 + 6\ O_2 + 6\ H_2O$$

| 6 carbon dioxide molecules | + | 12 water molecules | + | Light | → | 1 sugar molecule | + | 6 oxygen molecules | + | 6 water molecules |

Food production doesn't stop there. Plants use the sugar to build a lot of other molecules. They build other kinds of sugars with names like sucrose, dextrose, and fructose. They build **starches,** which store energy in potatoes and grains. They build oils, such as corn oil, sunflower oil, and olive oil.

Plants store energy as sugars, starches, and oils. When the plant needs them, it pulls them out of storage, turns them back into glucose, and sends the glucose to the cells. That's how plants survive at night and during winters.

Other organisms use the energy stored by plants. That includes you. When you eat a slice of bread or a baked potato, you are eating energy stored by a plant. When you eat lettuce and carrots, you are eating the sugars, starches, and all the cells made by plants. And when you take in food to nourish your cells, remember where the food came from. It started as carbon dioxide, water, and **sunlight.** It's really quite amazing when you stop to think about it. You are running on solar energy.

Review Questions

1. **What is sugar?**

2. **What raw materials do plants need to build sugar molecules? Where do those materials come from?**

3. **What is the role played by chlorophyll?**

4. **What are the products of photosynthesis? Where do they go?**

5. **Where do plants produce food?**

6. **You run on solar energy. How is that possible?**

LS2g. Students know plant and animal cells break down sugar to obtain energy, a process resulting in carbon dioxide (CO_2) and water (respiration).

Cellular Respiration

Cells work hard. They make useful molecules, exchange gases, send electric messages, and change shape. Cell activities require energy. The energy comes from sugar.

Cells break down large sugar molecules into molecules of water and carbon dioxide. This process of breaking down sugar is called **cellular respiration.** Cellular respiration releases energy that cells use to do what they do.

The equation for cellular respiration should look familiar. It is a lot like photosynthesis, but in reverse. Photosynthesis makes sugar and oxygen out of water and carbon dioxide. Cellular respiration makes water and carbon dioxide out of sugar and oxygen. The solar energy that goes into making sugar molecules comes out in a form useful to cells when the sugar is taken apart.

$$C_6H_{12}O_6 + 6\ O_2 \rightarrow 6\ CO_2 + 6\ H_2O + \text{Energy for cells}$$

| 1 sugar molecule | + | 6 oxygen molecules | → | 6 carbon dioxide molecules | + | 6 water molecules | + | Energy |

In cellular respiration, one sugar molecule reacts with six oxygen molecules to produce six carbon dioxide molecules and six water molecules. As the water molecules and carbon dioxide molecules form, energy is released to fuel cellular activities.

Do not confuse cellular respiration with breathing, which is also called respiration. Breathing brings oxygen to cells and carries carbon dioxide away from cells. Cellular respiration breaks down sugar to release energy.

Cellular Respiration in Humans

People, like all other animals, get the energy needed for cell activity from sugar. But we don't eat just sugar. We eat bread, meat, cabbage, beans, cheese, peaches, honey, potatoes, ice cream, carrots, corn, and thousands of other things. Humans are omnivores. That means we eat just about anything.

Some foods, like honey and peaches, are sweet because they contain a lot of sugar. Other foods, like potatoes and cheese, are not sweet. They contain little sugar. But potatoes and cheese provide energy for cells. Do you know how?

Humans digest food. The mouth, stomach, and intestines first break food into small bits. Then chemicals break down the bits into molecules. One of the molecules is sugar. The sugar goes into the blood for delivery to all the cells in your body.

What's in Food

Food is made of thousands of different substances. Those substances are called nutrients. Nutrients are the things cells use to stay alive and perform their functions.

Nutrients can be divided into six groups. All the substances in a group are similar chemically. The six nutrient groups are carbohydrates, proteins, fats, vitamins, minerals, and water.

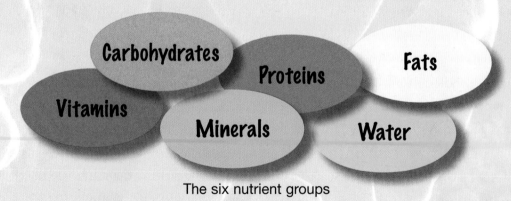

The six nutrient groups

Providing these six nutrients for your cells is called **nutrition.** People who do not have enough food, or the right kinds of food, suffer from malnutrition. Malnutrition can cause serious health problems if it continues for too long.

Good nutrition is a matter of eating good food. Good food means both enough food and food with good nutritional value. Nutritional food contains all of the nutrient groups in the right amounts. A diet that has too much of any one or two nutrients is not a good idea.

Food Groups

The United States Department of Agriculture (USDA) has divided foods into six **food groups.** They are grains, vegetables, fruits, oils, milk, and meat and beans.

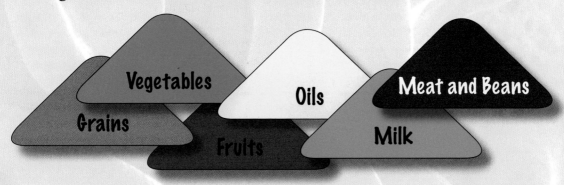

The six USDA food groups

Food groups are different than nutrient groups. Food groups are based partly on the main nutrients in them and partly on where the food comes from. For instance, grains are all grass seeds and are mostly carbohydrate. But they contain some protein and fat, and they have vitamins and minerals. Meats and beans have high protein content, but beans also have carbohydrate, and meat has fat.

The key to healthy nutrition is eating the right amount of food in all six food groups. The USDA **food pyramid** shows the recommended amount of food in each food group. You should eat more foods from the wide sections. A healthy diet includes more grains, fruits, vegetables, and milk, and less oil and meat. Eating suggested amounts in each group provides a balanced diet.

| Grain | Vegetable | Fruit | Oil | Milk | Meat |

121

The pyramid shape is important, too. You can draw a line across the pyramid near the bottom and another one across the top. The two lines represent the nutritional needs of two different people. The bottom line could be a college football player. The upper line could be a fifth-grade student.

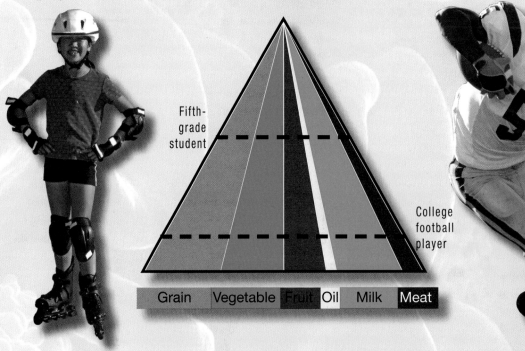

Fifth-grade student

College football player

| Grain | Vegetable | Fruit | Oil | Milk | Meat |

The football player's line is longer. He needs a lot more food to nourish his cells because he is a lot bigger and uses a lot of energy playing football. The fifth-grade student's line is shorter because she doesn't need as much food. She is smaller and does things that don't take as much energy.

Even though the student eats less than the football player, they both eat more in the grain group than any other group. And they both eat only a little bit in the oil group. The amount of oil the football player eats is larger than the amount of oil the student eats. That's because he eats more in every food group to make sure all his cells are well nourished.

Food around the World

The USDA food pyramid is designed for people living in the United States. Other parts of the world have different food pyramids. These pyramids are based on foods that are common in those parts of the world. As you look at the food pyramids for Latin American, East Asian, and Mediterranean countries, you will see similarities to the USDA pyramid.

Latin American Diet

Latin America includes Mexico and Central and South America. The foundation of Latin American nutrition is fruits, vegetables, grains (particularly corn), beans, and potatoes. Protein comes mostly from beans, fish, and poultry. Meat, eggs, and sweets are eaten in small amounts.

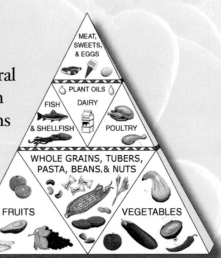

Guatemalan marketplace

Sharing a meal featuring the food of a typical
Latin American diet

East Asian Diet

East Asia includes China, Thailand, Vietnam, Japan, and Korea. The traditional East Asian diet is grain oriented. Rice is the foundation of Asian nutrition. It is eaten with vegetables every day. Protein comes from beans and fish. Eggs, meat, and sweets are eaten in small amounts, and milk is not an important part of the Asian diet.

MEAT

SWEETS

EGGS & POULTRY

FISH & SHELLFISH or DAIRY

VEGETABLE OILS

FRUITS | LEGUMES, SEEDS, & NUTS | VEGETABLES

RICE, NOODLES, BREADS, MILLET, CORN, & OTHER WHOLE GRAINS

Sharing a meal featuring the food of a typical East Asian diet

A floating market near Bangkok, Thailand

Mediterranean Diet

The countries along the north side of the Mediterranean Sea include Spain, France, Italy, and Greece. Wheat, eaten in the form of bread and pasta, is central in the Mediterranean diet. Fruits, vegetables, cheese, and olive oil are common. Red meat and sweets are eaten in small amounts.

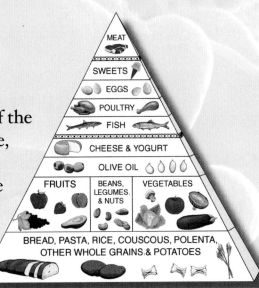

Buying produce at a vegetable stand in Venice, Italy

Sharing a meal featuring the food of a typical Mediterranean diet

Review Questions

1. Why do people eat food?

2. How do your cells get energy from the food you eat?

3. How do plant cells get the energy they need?

4. What happens during cellular respiration?

LS2g. Students know plant and animal cells break down sugar to obtain energy, a process resulting in carbon dioxide (CO_2) and water (respiration).

Living with Diabetes

Diabetes is a disease that affects the body's ability to use glucose correctly. Glucose is the sugar that provides energy to cells. The **pancreas** is a gland that normally produces insulin. **Insulin** controls the amount of glucose in the blood. Type I **diabetes** is a disease that causes the pancreas to stop making insulin. Without insulin, too much glucose builds up in the bloodstream. If it isn't treated, diabetes can cause blindness, kidney disease, heart disease, coma, and even death.

Diabetes affects people of all ages, including children. Most children with this disease have type I diabetes. Type I diabetes is also known as insulin-dependent diabetes. Children with type I diabetes must take insulin to survive. They must also carefully monitor the foods they eat, to make sure that they don't have too much sugar in their blood.

Robin Reitzes

Jon Reitzes

Robin and Jon Reitzes are a sister and brother who have been living with type I diabetes since they were very young. At the time of this interview, Robin was a 24-year-old graduate student in New York. And Jon was a 20-year-old college student in Missouri.

Q: How old were you when you were diagnosed?

RR: I was 13 months old when I was first diagnosed. At the time, I became very ill. I was vomiting, lethargic, and losing weight. I was put in the hospital and was very close to dying. Finally the diabetes was diagnosed.

JR: I was 8 months old when I was diagnosed. My mother recognized the symptoms and took me to the hospital.

Q: How was your life different from other boys and girls?

RR: I never felt any different from any of the other kids in school. I don't remember having a low blood sugar reaction in elementary school. As a child, I always knew when my blood sugar was going low. I had to have snack time, but so did the other kids. The only difference was not being able to eat cupcakes. Instead I would go to school with an apple.

JR: When I was very little, I never even thought about having diabetes. I think I started really thinking about it when I was in the second or third grade. I remember very clearly sitting on the counter and crying about it. But that was probably a result of my blood sugar being low.

Q: When did you start giving yourself insulin shots?

RR: Mom gave me my shots until I was 9 or 10. After that, I was glad to be able to take care of myself and be independent. Today I take about three or four shots a day.

JR: I was on my own with the insulin by the age of 8 or 9. Of course, my mom always checked to make sure everything was OK. We kept logbooks.

Q: Is it difficult to give yourself insulin shots?

JR: People always ask, "How can you do this? Doesn't it hurt?" You do it because you have to. It's going to save your life. People get up, brush their teeth, and go. I just have another step.

Q: Does exercise help you control your diabetes?

RR: Exercise is the best thing that ever happened. It helps keep my blood sugar down, helps the insulin work more efficiently, and helps me maintain a healthy weight. I try to exercise 4 to 5 days a week.

JR: I was very active in high school. Wrestling, cross country, lacrosse. I never had high blood sugar when I was wrestling. Now that I'm in college, I have a heavy workload. But I still try to exercise whenever I can. I rollerblade or walk a couple of miles to class whenever possible. Everything works better, your mind and body, when you exercise.

Q: What is your diet like? Do you have a nutrition plan?

RR: I can eat all foods in moderation. For example, I'm having a little ice cream tonight because I exercised for 2 hours today. In my mind, I keep track of what I eat. The important thing is to keep my blood sugar at a normal, healthy level. The better I do this, the healthier I am.

JR: I pretty much eat what I like. But when food can make you physically ill, sometimes you go for it, and a lot of times you don't. You look at food in a completely different way. Moderation is the key. You have to understand that there are immediate consequences to eating. I can live the life I want as long as I balance insulin, diet, and exercise.

Q: What is the worst thing about having diabetes?

RR: Where do I start? I think the worst thing is that I can't be spontaneous. I must know when to eat and when to exercise. I'm always on a schedule. I like to travel, but I worry about losing my insulin. I'm always double- and triple-checking my bag. In my pocketbook, I always have to carry my blood sugar monitor, insulin, syringes, and other stuff.

Q: What would you like to tell kids who have diabetes?

RR: Take good care of yourself. The more you neglect it, the worse you feel. A lot of kids in our town had it. You'd see kids not taking care of themselves, not doing their shots. That's when you see the worst cases. You can manage your diabetes and live a normal, healthy life.

JR: There are two ways to look at diabetes. You can view it as a challenge, with your goal being to become a healthy person. Or you can give up. You have to become master of yourself very early on. Don't waste time waiting for something to happen. Don't wait for a cure or hope for this or that. Take responsibility for yourself. Diabetes is a part of you, but it doesn't need to consume you.

Q: How can kids without diabetes support those who do have this condition?

RR: They should treat kids with diabetes normally. It's hard enough to be a kid with all the teasing that goes on. Diabetes is treatable, and it's not contagious.

JR: If your friend has diabetes, be sensitive to his needs if he's going to hang out with you. Nothing means more than a friend who is concerned, who takes a second out of his day to make sure everything is OK.

Summary: Sugar and Cells

Living cells are always doing things. Doing things requires energy. To stay alive, every living cell needs a steady supply of energy.

The source of energy for most living organisms on Earth is the Sun. Energy in the form of light falls on Earth all day. That light, however, is not in a form that cells can use. Light energy has to be changed into another energy form before cells can use it.

The energy form that cells can use is sugar. Plants can change light energy into sugar. Here's how they do it.

Many plant cells, particularly the cells in leaves, contain **chlorophyll.** Chlorophyll absorbs light energy. Carbon dioxide and water combine with the energy absorbed by the chlorophyll to build sugar and release oxygen.

Building sugar from carbon dioxide and water with light energy is called **photosynthesis.** This is the basic equation for photosynthesis.

$$6\ CO_2 + 12\ H_2O + \text{Solar energy} \rightarrow C_6H_{12}O_6 + 6\ O_2 + 6\ H_2O$$

| 6 carbon dioxide molecules | + | 12 water molecules | + | Light | → | 1 sugar molecule | + | 6 oxygen molecules | + | 6 water molecules |

Six molecules of carbon dioxide (CO_2), twelve molecules of water (H_2O), and energy from **sunlight** are used to build one molecule of sugar ($C_6H_{12}O_6$), six molecules of oxygen gas (O_2), and six molecules of water.

The sugar made during photosynthesis is **glucose.** One glucose molecule is made of 24 atoms attached to one another with bonds. The solar energy absorbed by the chlorophyll is used to build the glucose molecule.

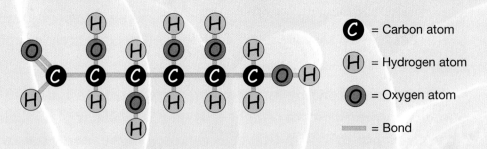

C = Carbon atom

H = Hydrogen atom

O = Oxygen atom

= Bond

Green plant cells change light energy (sunshine) into chemical energy (glucose). Those same cells use the energy in the sugar to do their work. And the sugar is transported to other cells that don't make sugar. This is an important idea. Plants make food for their own use. The food they make allows them to survive.

Animal cells cannot make sugar. But animal cells need sugar to survive. Animals deal with this problem by eating plants and other organisms for food. The food that animals eat is digested, turning it into sugar and other nutrients. Blood transports the sugar to all the animals' cells. The cells use the sugar for energy to do the things they need to do.

Plant cells and animal cells break down sugar molecules in a process called **cellular respiration.** Cellular respiration breaks sugar and oxygen molecules into water and carbon dioxide.

$$C_6H_{12}O_6 + 6\ O_2 \rightarrow 6\ CO_2 + 6\ H_2O + \text{Energy for cells}$$

| 1 sugar molecule | + | 6 oxygen molecules | → | 6 carbon dioxide molecules | + | 6 water molecules | + | Energy |

One sugar molecule and six oxygen molecules break down into six carbon dioxide molecules, six water molecules, and energy. The solar energy that goes into making sugar molecules comes out in a form that cells use when they take sugar apart.

Summary Questions

Now is a good time to review what you have recorded in your science notebook. Think about the connection between photosynthesis and cellular respiration, particularly how the connection involves energy.

1. What does chlorophyll do?

2. What raw materials do plants use to make sugar?

3. Why do plants make sugar?

4. What happens to sugar when it is used in cells?

5. How do your cells obtain energy from the Sun?

California Science Standards

LS2f. Students know plants use carbon dioxide (CO_2) and energy from sunlight to build molecules of sugar and release oxygen.

LS2g. Students know plant and animal cells break down sugar to obtain energy, a process resulting in carbon dioxide (CO_2) and water (respiration).

Vocabulary

chlorophyll

photosynthesis

sunlight

glucose

cellular respiration

Extensions

Math Problem of the Week

Three classes of nutrients provide energy. They are carbohydrate, protein, and fat. Food energy is measured in calories. You get different numbers of calories from different nutrients.

1 gram of carbohydrate = 4 calories (Cal)

1 gram of protein   = 4 calories (Cal)

1 gram of fat   = 9 calories (Cal)

Bif went to a baseball game. He ate a hot dog, a bag of chips, and a soda. When he got home, he wondered how many calories he got from his fast-food meal. He looked up the average calories for the items he ate. The data are shown in the table.

Food item	Protein (g) (4 Cal/g)	Carbohydrate (g) (4 Cal/g)	Fat (g) (9 Cal/g)
Hot dog	8	20	16
Potato chips	4	31	20
Soda	0	36	0

1. How many calories was Bif's meal?

2. Bif was happy with the total calories in his meal. But he wants to have only 30% of his calories from fat. Does fat provide more than 30% of the calories in Bif's meal?

3. If Bif has too much fat in his meal, how many grams of fat will he have to remove? How many grams of carbohydrate and/or protein will he have to add?

Learning More about Living Systems

Find Out about the Man with a Hole in His Stomach

Dr. William Beaumont was a physician. In 1822 he had a patient with a gunshot wound. The man was left with a small hole in his stomach. Find out how Dr. Beaumont studied the digestive process with this patient over the next 10 years.

Research Other Organs Involved in Digestion

Other organs help the digestive process. These include the liver, gallbladder, and pancreas. The liver produces bile to break down fats. The gallbladder stores bile. The pancreas produces enzymes that aid in digestion. Read more about these organs, what they do, and health problems associated with them.

Research Dialysis

Find out about dialysis, the medical procedure that filters blood when kidneys don't function properly.

Research Asthma

Asthma is a respiratory condition that many children have in the United States. A person with asthma has trouble breathing and can have coughing attacks. Find out more about asthma.

Find Out about the Hearts of Other Animals

Mammals have hearts with four chambers. What about birds, reptiles, fish, and insects? Draw labeled diagrams of the hearts and circulatory systems of other animals.

Diagram an Organ System

Make a detailed, labeled diagram of one or more of the organ systems you have studied.

Study a Cross Section of Wood

Get a cross section of a log, branch, or twig from a tree. Study the pattern of rings in the wood. The concentric rings (those with a common center) are layers of xylem that have fallen into disuse. Find the active layer of xylem, which is just under the tree's bark.

Investigate Flower Cells

Are flowers made of cells? If so, do they need water? Design an investigation to find out. HINT: A white carnation would be a good flower to experiment with.

What Is Maple Syrup?

Write a report about how to make maple syrup. Be sure to discuss how the two transport systems of vascular plants figure in the story.

Test Various Sugars

Conduct the sugar test on several sugars. Try powdered sugar, brown sugar, corn syrup, maple syrup, honey, and molasses.

Test Liquids

Design a method for testing the sugar content of liquids, such as sodas and fruit juices.

Test Sugar Substitutes

Obtain several brands of sugar substitutes or artificial sweeteners. Test them, using the sugar test. You may be surprised by the results. Be sure to read the labels carefully.

Calculate Percentage of Sugar

Do the sugar test on a food sample. Let the test run until all the sugar in the sample changes into gas. Do the same thing with an equal-size sample of pure sugar. Calculate the percentage of sugar in the food sample. Divide the volume of gas produced by the unknown, by the volume of gas produced by sugar. Multiply the result by 100.

Find Sugars in Products

In chemistry, sugars are always identified by the suffix *-ose*. The sugar with which we are most familiar is sucrose. Other common sugars include glucose, dextrose, fructose, and lactose. Read product labels to find and list as many sugars as you can identify.

Develop Your Own Food Pyramid

The United States Department of Agriculture has developed a food pyramid. It provides information about the amount of food to eat in each of six food groups. It also incorporates other factors, such as body weight, physical activity, and age. Customize your own food pyramid using the USDA website called MyPyramid.gov.

http://www.mypyramid.gov/

Life Sciences Glossary

Artery   A blood vessel that carries blood from the heart to the body.

Bladder   The organ that holds urine until it is eliminated.

Blade   The flat part of a leaf.

Bolus   A wad of food.

Botanist   A scientist who studies plants.

Capillary   The smallest blood vessel. Gases, nutrients, and wastes are exchanged between capillaries and cells.

Carbohydrate   A group of nutrients that provides energy; sugars and starches.

Carbon dioxide   A waste gas produced during cellular respiration. Plants use carbon dioxide during photosynthesis to make food.

Cell   The basic unit of life.

Cellular respiration   The process by which energy for life is released from food in cells.

Cellular waste   Chemicals produced by cells that must be removed.

Chlorophyll   A molecule that absorbs red and blue light and reflects green light.

Circulate   To move in or flow through in a circle.

Circulatory system   The system of blood vessels and organs that transports blood to all the cells in the body.

Classification   The process by which scientists identify and organize objects and organisms, such as plants.

Classify   To identify and organize according to similar properties or other criteria.

Colon   The large intestine where solid waste is compacted in preparation for elimination.

Cytoplasm   The liquid that fills living cells.

Diabetes   A disease in which the body cannot process sugar efficiently.

Digestion   The process of breaking down food into nutrients that can be used by cells.

Digestive system   The system of organs and structures responsible for the digestion of food. The digestive system includes the teeth, mouth, esophagus, stomach, small intestine, large intestine, and colon.

Energy   What cells need to do work.

Esophagus   The tube connecting the mouth and the stomach.

Excretory system   The system, which includes the kidneys and bladder, that eliminates waste.

Fat   A group of nutrients that provides energy and building blocks for the development of some body systems.

Food group   The six groups designated by the United States Department of Agriculture (USDA) for a healthy diet. The six food groups are grains, vegetables, fruits, oils, milk, and meat and beans.

Food pyramid   An illustration that shows the recommended amounts of food in each food group for a healthy diet.

Glucose   A sugar found in food; the sugar broken down in cells to release energy.

Heart   A muscular organ that pumps blood.

Insulin   A substance that controls the amount of glucose in the body.

Intestine   A part of the digestive system. The small intestine absorbs nutrients from digested food. The large intestine removes water from solid waste.

Kidney   An organ that filters and cleans the blood.

Large intestine   The part of the digestive system between the small intestine and the rectum where water is removed from the solid waste.

Left atrium   The upper chamber on the left side of the heart.

Left ventricle   The lower chamber on the left side of the heart.

Lung   The organ in animals where gases, such as oxygen and carbon dioxide, pass between the atmosphere and the blood.

Margin   The edge of a leaf.

Membrane   The outside of a living cell.

Mineral   A nutrient that xylem transports to the cells in a vascular plant.

Mouth   A body opening where an animal takes in food.

Multicellular organism   An organism composed of many cells.

Nutrient   A chemical found in food that helps keep an organism alive and active.

Nutrition   The process of providing nutrients for cells.

Oxygen   A waste gas produced by plants during photosynthesis, which is used by all plants and animals during cellular respiration.

Palmate   A leaf vein pattern in which there are several veins that all start at one point near the base. The veins look like the fingers of a hand.

Pancreas   The gland in the body that produces insulin.

Parallel   A leaf vein pattern in which the veins are straight lines all running in the same direction.

Phloem   The long cells through which nutrients, such as sugars, are distributed in a plant.

Photosynthesis   The process by which green plants make sugar from carbon dioxide and water in the presence of light.

Pinnate   A leaf vein pattern that looks like a feather. There is one main vein that has smaller veins branching off sideways from it.

Protein A group of nutrients that provides energy and building blocks for growth and repair of body tissues.

Respiratory system The system of lungs and connecting tubes that transports oxygen to the red blood cells and gets rid of carbon dioxide.

Right atrium The upper chamber on the right side of the heart.

Right ventricle The lower chamber on the right side of the heart.

Saliva The liquid produced in the mouth that aids digestion.

Sap A sugar-rich liquid transported by phloem.

Small intestine The part of the digestive system between the stomach and large intestine that absorbs nutrients from digested food.

Specialized structure A structure used primarily for one purpose.

Starch Chemicals produced by plants to store food.

Stomach The organ where food is reduced to mush by acid and muscle activity.

Sugar The nutrient that cells use for energy.

Sunlight Light from the Sun.

Teeth Hard structures in the mouth used for cutting, biting, and chewing food.

Tissue A group of similar cells working together to perform a function.

Transport To move or carry.

Urine Liquid waste produced by kidneys.

Variable Anything you can change in an experiment that might affect the outcome.

Vascular bundle The group of xylem tubes and phloem tubes in a vascular plant.

Vascular plant   A plant with an internal system of tubes for transporting nutrients to its roots, stems, and leaves.

Vein   The blood vessel that carries blood from the body to the heart.

Waste disposal   The removal of unusable material.

Water   A liquid earth material made of hydrogen and oxygen.

Xylem   The hollow cells of a plant that transport water and minerals to plant cells.

Water Planet

Earth Sciences
Table of Contents

Water Planet

A Tour of the Solar System

Make believe you are coming to the **solar system** as a stranger. You are on a tour. There is a tour guide to provide information. You have a window to look out. The tour is about to start. What will you see?

The first view of the solar system is from space. From here the whole solar system can be seen. The most surprising thing is that the solar system is mostly empty. The matter is concentrated in tiny dots. And the dots are far apart. Most of the dots are **planets.** From far away, that is what you see.

There is a **star** in the center of the solar system. Four small planets **orbit** pretty close to the star. These are the rocky **terrestrial planets.**

Next there is a region of small bits of matter orbiting the star. This is the **asteroid** belt.

Out farther, four big gas planets orbit the star. These are the **gas giants.**

Beyond the gas giants is a huge region of different-size icy chunks of matter called the **Kuiper Belt.** Some of the chunks are big enough to be planets. Others have orbits that send them flying through the rest of the solar system. That's all that can be seen from out in space.

Sizes and distances of solar-system objects are not drawn to scale.

The Sun

The **Sun** is a star. It is just like the stars you can see in the night sky. The Sun is at the center of the solar system. Everything else in the solar system orbits the Sun. The Sun rules.

Earth

The Sun is an average star. It is much like millions of other stars in the **Milky Way** galaxy. The Sun formed about 5 billion years ago. A cloud of gas began to spin. As it spun, it formed a sphere. The sphere got smaller and smaller. As it got smaller, it got hotter. Eventually the sphere got so hot it started to radiate light and heat. A star was born.

The Sun is made mostly of **hydrogen** (72%) and **helium** (26%). And it is huge. The diameter is about 1,384,000 kilometers (860,000 miles). The diameter is the distance from one side of the Sun to the other through the center. That's about 109 times the diameter of Earth. (See Earth compared to the Sun at the bottom of the picture on the left.)

The Sun is incredibly hot. Scientists have figured out that the temperature at the center of the Sun is 15,000,000°C (27,000,000°F). The temperature of the Sun's surface is lower, about 5,500°C (10,000°F). Hydrogen atoms constantly combine to form helium atoms in **thermonuclear reactions.** These reactions create heat and light energy. About 3.6 tons of the Sun's **mass** is being changed into heat and light every second. This energy radiates out from the Sun in all directions. A small amount of it falls on Earth.

Another name for the Sun is Sol. That's why the whole system of planets is called the solar system. The solar system is named for the ruling star. The reason the Sun rules is its size. The Sun has 99.8% of the total mass of the solar system. All the other solar-system objects travel around the Sun in **predictable** almost-circular paths called orbits. The most obvious objects orbiting the Sun are the planets.

Terrestrial Planets

The terrestrial planets are the four planets closest to the Sun. The terrestrial planets are small and rocky.

Relative sizes of the terrestrial planets

Mercury

Mercury is closest to the Sun. Mercury is smaller than Earth and has no **satellite** (moon). By human standards, it is an uninviting place. Mercury is very hot on the side facing the Sun and very cold on the dark side. It has no atmosphere or water.

Mercury is covered with craters. The **craters** are the result of thousands of collisions with objects flying through space. The surface of Mercury looks a lot like Earth's Moon.

Planet Mercury is closest to the Sun.

Venus

Venus is the second planet from the Sun. Venus is about the same size as Earth and has no satellites. The surface of Venus is very hot all the time. It is hot enough to melt lead, making it one of the hottest places in the solar system.

There is no liquid water on Venus. But Venus does have an atmosphere of carbon dioxide. The dense, cloudy atmosphere makes it impossible to see the planet's surface. Modern radar, however, allows scientists to take pictures through the clouds. We now know that the surface of Venus is dry, cracked, and covered with volcanoes.

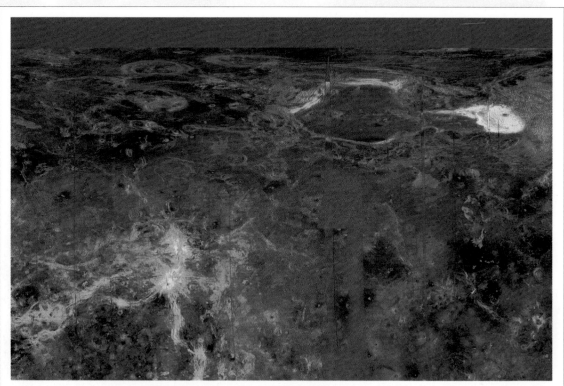

The surface of Venus is hot and cratered.

Earth

Earth is the third planet from the Sun. Earth has a moderate (mild) temperature all the time. It has an atmosphere of nitrogen and oxygen, and it has liquid water. As far as we know, Earth is the only place in the universe that has life. Earth also has one large satellite called the **Moon,** or Luna. The Moon orbits Earth once a month. The Moon is responsible for the tides in Earth's oceans. The Moon is the only **extraterrestrial** place humans have visited.

Moon

Earth is 150 million kilometers (93 million miles) from the Sun. This is a huge distance. It's hard to imagine that distance, but think about this. Sit in one end zone of a football field and curl up into a ball. You are the Sun. A friend goes to the other end zone and holds up the eraser from a pencil. That's Earth. Get the idea? Earth is tiny, and it is a long distance from the Sun. Still, the solar energy that reaches Earth provides the right amount of energy for life as we know it.

Mars

Mars is the fourth planet from the Sun and has two small satellites, Phobos and Deimos. Mars is a little like Earth, except it is smaller, colder, and drier. There are some places on Mars that are like Death Valley in California. Other places on Mars are more like Antarctica and the volcanoes of Hawaii.

Mars is sometimes called the Red Planet because of its red soil. The soil contains iron oxide, or rust. The iron oxide in the soil tells scientists that Mars probably had liquid water at one time. But liquid water has not been on Mars for 3.5 billion years. It has frozen water in polar ice caps that grow and shrink with the seasons on Mars.

Mars is the next likely place humans will visit. But exploring Mars will not be easy. Humans can't breathe the thin atmosphere of carbon dioxide. And explorers will need to wear life-support spacesuits for protection against the cold.

Several robotic landers, such as *Viking, Spirit, Opportunity,* and *Sojourner,* have observed Mars and sent back information about the surface and possibility of water. There is evidence that there is a lot of frozen water just under the surface.

Water frost on the surface of Mars

151

Asteroids

Beyond the orbit of Mars there are millions of chunks of rock and iron called asteroids. They all orbit the Sun in a region called the asteroid belt. The asteroid belt is like the boundary of the terrestrial planets. The planets farther out are quite different from the terrestrial planets.

Asteroid Ida with satellite Dactyl

Some asteroids even have moons. When the spacecraft *Galileo* flew past asteroid Ida in 1993, scientists were surprised to find it had a satellite. They named the tiny moon Dactyl. The biggest asteroid is Ceres. It is about 960 kilometers (600 miles) around.

Gas Giants

The next four planets are the gas giants. They do not have rocky surfaces like the terrestrial planets. So there is no place to land or walk around on them. They are much bigger than the terrestrial planets. What we have learned about the gas giants has come from probes sent out to fly by and orbit around them. Even though the gas giants are all made of gas, each one is different.

Relative sizes of the gas giants

Jupiter

Jupiter is the fifth planet from the Sun. Jupiter is the largest planet in the solar system. It is 11 times larger in diameter than Earth. Sixty-three moons have been found to orbit Jupiter. The four largest moons are Ganymede, Callisto, Io, and Europa.

Jupiter's atmosphere is cold and poisonous. It is mostly hydrogen and helium. The stripes and swirls on Jupiter's surface are cold, windy clouds of ammonia and water. Its Great Red Spot is a giant storm as wide as three Earths. This storm has been raging for hundreds of years. On Jupiter, the atmospheric pressure is so strong it squishes gas into liquid. Jupiter's atmosphere could crush a metal spaceship like a paper cup.

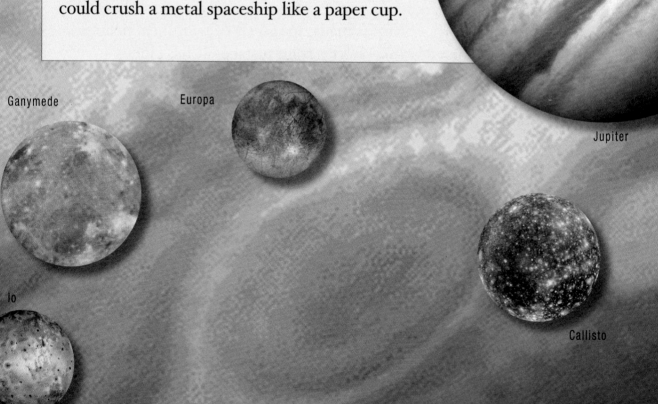

Ganymede

Europa

Jupiter

Io

Callisto

Saturn

Saturn

Saturn is the sixth planet from the Sun. Saturn is the second biggest planet and is very cold. There are at least 46 satellites orbiting Saturn. Saturn is made up mostly of hydrogen, helium, and methane. It doesn't have a solid surface. It has clouds and storms like Jupiter, but they are harder to see because they move so fast. Winds in Saturn's upper atmosphere reach 1,825 kilometers per hour (1,135 miles per hour).

The most dramatic feature of Saturn is its ring system. The largest ring reaches out 200,000 kilometers (125,000 miles) from Saturn's surface. The rings are made of billions of small chunks of ice and rock. All the gas giants have rings, but the others are not as spectacular as Saturn's.

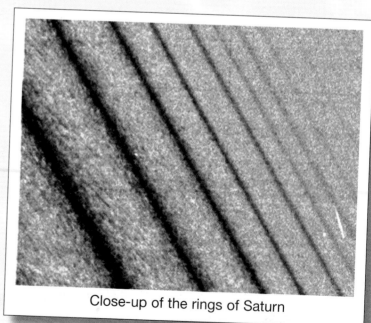

Close-up of the rings of Saturn

Uranus

Uranus is the seventh planet from the Sun. Uranus has 27 moons and 11 rings. Uranus is very cold and windy, and would be poisonous to humans. It is smaller and colder than Saturn.

Uranus has clouds that are extremely cold at the top. Below the cloud tops there is a layer of extremely hot water, ammonia, and methane. Near its core, Uranus heats up to 4,982°C (9,000°F). Uranus appears blue because of the methane gas in its atmosphere.

Neptune

Uranus

Neptune

Neptune is the eighth planet from the Sun. Neptune has 13 moons and 4 thin rings. Neptune is the smallest of the gas giants, but is still the fourth largest planet in the solar system.

Neptune is made mostly of hydrogen and helium with some methane. Neptune may be the windiest planet in the solar system. Winds rip through the clouds at more than 2,000 kilometers per hour (1,200 miles per hour). Scientists think there might be an ocean of super-hot water under Neptune's cold clouds. It does not boil away, because of the incredible pressure.

Kuiper Belt

Pluto

Out beyond the gas giants is a disk-shaped zone of icy objects called the Kuiper Belt. Some of the objects are fairly large. **Pluto** is one of the Kuiper Belt objects. Some scientists considered Pluto a planet because it is massive enough to pull itself into a sphere. Others did not consider Pluto a planet. To them, Pluto was just one of the large pieces of debris in the Kuiper Belt. Scientists now call Pluto a dwarf planet.

Pluto has a thin atmosphere. It is so cold on Pluto that the atmosphere actually freezes and falls to Pluto's surface when it is farthest from the Sun. Even though Pluto is smaller than Earth's Moon, it has its own satellite. It is called Charon and is about half the size of Pluto.

Pluto and its moon Charon

Eris

In July 2005, astronomers at the California Institute of Technology announced the discovery of a new planet-like object. It is called Eris. Like Pluto, Eris is a Kuiper Belt object and a dwarf planet. But Eris is more than twice as far away from the Sun as Pluto! The picture to the right is an artist's idea of what the Sun would look like from a position close to Eris.

A painting showing that the Sun would look like a bright star from Eris

Comets

Comets are big chunks of ice, rock, and gas. Sometimes comets are compared to dirty snowballs. Scientists think comets might have valuable information about the origins of the solar system.

Comets orbit the Sun in long, oval paths. Most of them travel way beyond the orbit of Pluto. A comet's trip around the Sun can take hundreds or even millions of years, depending on its orbit. A comet's tail shows up as it nears the Sun and begins to warm. The gases and dust that form the comet's tail always point away from the Sun.

Comets have been called dirty snowballs.

Comet orbits can cross those of the planets. In July 1994 a large comet, named Comet Shoemaker-Levy 9, was on a collision course with Jupiter. As it got close to Jupiter, the comet broke into 21 pieces.

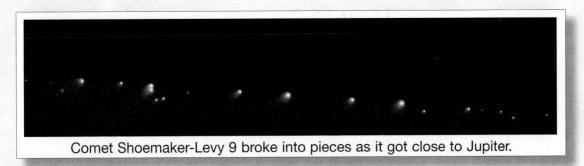

Comet Shoemaker-Levy 9 broke into pieces as it got close to Jupiter.

The pieces slammed into Jupiter for a week. Each impact created a crater in Jupiter's surface larger than planet Earth.

Two of the 21 larger than Earth-size craters on Jupiter

Review Questions

1. What is the Sun and what is it made of?

2. What is the solar system?

3. Which planets are terrestrial planets? Which planets are gas giants?

4. What is the Kuiper Belt and what is found there?

5. Which planet has the most moons orbiting it?

6. How are asteroids and comets alike and different?

ES5a. Students know the Sun, an average star, is the central and largest body in the solar system and is composed primarily of hydrogen and helium.

Ramon E. Lopez

As strange as it may sound, there is weather in space. But it's not weather like we have on Earth. There are no clouds, hurricanes, or snowstorms in space. Space weather is the result of activities on the Sun. The Sun is always radiating energy into the solar system. The regular flow of light and gases is called **solar wind.** But what happens when the Sun goes through a period of violent solar flares? That's what Dr. Ramon E. Lopez (1959–) studies.

Ramon E. Lopez

Solar flares, which are huge solar explosions, send intense blasts of electrified gas into Earth's atmosphere. The blasts can produce electric effects in the atmosphere and on Earth's surface. The electricity can disable satellites orbiting Earth and interfere with radio transmissions and cell-phone operation. Space weather can cause blackouts over large areas.

Sun with a large flare

Lopez and his team understand how space weather can damage communication and navigation systems. And they understand how important these systems are to modern society. Will Lopez be able to predict the space weather? Will he be able to warn the world when a dangerous storm is coming from the Sun? Lopez believes that the team he works with may be able to develop a computer program to predict space weather about 30 minutes before it hits Earth. And that may be just long enough to take steps to protect communication and navigation systems from damage.

ES5c. Students know the path of a planet around the Sun is due to the gravitational attraction between the Sun and the planet.

Why Doesn't Earth Fly Off into Space?

Earth travels around the Sun in a predictable, almost-circular path once a year. That's a distance of about 942 million kilometers (584 million miles) each year. That's an incredible 2.6 million kilometers (1.6 million miles) each day! That's fast.

One important thing to know about objects in motion is that they travel only in straight lines. Objects don't change direction or follow curved paths unless a force pushes or pulls them in a new direction. If nothing pushed or pulled on Earth, it would fly off into space in a straight line.

Sun

But Earth doesn't fly straight off into space. Earth travels in a circular path around the Sun. In order to travel a circular path, Earth has to change direction all the time. Something has to push or pull Earth to change its direction. What is pushing or pulling our planet Earth? **Gravity.**

Gravity is the force of attraction between masses. The Sun is a mass. Earth is a mass. The force of attraction between the Sun and Earth pulls hard enough to change Earth's direction of travel.

Remember the string-and-ball demonstration? The hand pulled on the string. The string pulled on the ball. The ball traveled in a circular orbit. Gravity is like the string. The **gravitational attraction** between the Sun and Earth pulls on Earth, changing its direction of travel. That's why Earth travels in a circular orbit around the Sun.

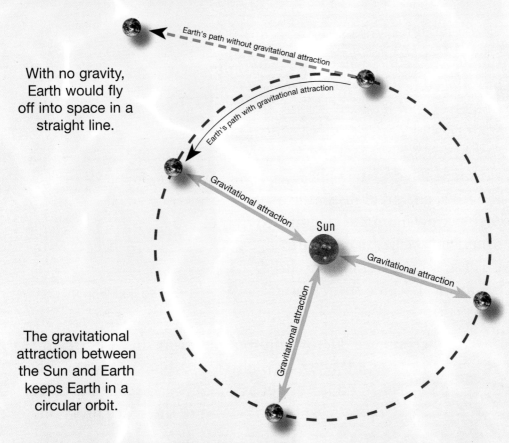

Earth's path without gravitational attraction

With no gravity, Earth would fly off into space in a straight line.

Earth's path with gravitational attraction

Gravitational attraction

Sun

Gravitational attraction

Gravitational attraction

The gravitational attraction between the Sun and Earth keeps Earth in a circular orbit.

Sun's gravity keeps all the planets in their orbits. Otherwise, the planets would fly in straight lines right out of the solar system.

Review Questions

1. **Why do planets stay in orbit around the Sun?**

2. **How is a ball on a string like a planet in its orbit?**

3. **What keeps the Moon in its orbit around Earth?**

INVESTIGATION 1

ES5c. Students know the path of a planet around the Sun is due to the gravitational attraction between the Sun and the planet.

Mae Jemison: Astronaut

Mae Jemison, astronaut

Dr. Mae Jemison (1956–) was born in Decatur, Alabama. She moved to Chicago, Illinois, as a child, where an uncle introduced her to **astronomy.** In high school Jemison began reading books on astronomy and space travel. She was only 16 years old when she entered college. She earned degrees in chemical engineering and African and Afro-American studies from Stanford University. She went on to earn her medical degree from Cornell University.

After becoming a doctor, Jemison spent time in western Africa as a Peace Corps physician. But she continued to think about astronomy and space travel. She wanted to be part of the space program.

The official patch of shuttle mission STS-47

Jemison was admitted into the astronaut program in 1987. On September 12, 1992, Jemison became the first African-American woman in space. She was a science mission specialist on the space shuttle *Endeavour.* Jemison conducted experiments to find out more about the effects of being in space. She studied motion sickness, calcium loss in bones, and weightlessness.

Space shuttle mission STS-47 was the 50th space shuttle flight, but only the second flight for the *Endeavour*. The shuttle was in space for 8 days. During those 8 days, Jemison orbited Earth 127 times at an altitude of 307 kilometers (191 miles). The shuttle traveled 5,234,950 kilometers (3,245,669 miles).

Does the space shuttle actually fly in space? Not really. It orbits Earth in the upper atmosphere. In the picture to the right, you can see how close the shuttle is to Earth's surface when it is in orbit. What keeps the shuttle in orbit?

Space shuttle orbit

The space shuttle in orbit

Again, gravity. The shuttle travels very fast. Earth's gravity pulls on the shuttle, constantly changing the shuttle's direction of travel. Engineers from the National Aeronautics and Space Administration (NASA) have figured out exactly how fast the shuttle must travel and how high it must be above Earth's surface. They know how strong the force of gravity is. With these data, the space shuttle stays in orbit until the astronauts change the shuttle's speed. Then gravity pulls the shuttle back to Earth. Mission complete.

Summary: Solar System

The **Milky Way** galaxy has hundreds of billions of **stars.** We live just 150 million kilometers (93 million miles) from one of them. That star is Sol, our **Sun.**

The Sun is not alone. **Planets, satellites, asteroids, comets,** and other objects travel in **orbits** around the Sun. The Sun and all the bodies that circle it make up the **solar system.**

The Sun

The Sun is by far the largest object in the solar system. It accounts for 99.8% of the mass in the whole solar system. And the Sun is about 109 times bigger than **Earth** in diameter. But unlike Earth, the Sun is made mostly of **hydrogen** (72%) and **helium** (26%). The light and heat radiating from the Sun are created as hydrogen atoms combine to make helium.

The Sun is an average star.

The Planets

Planets are large natural objects that orbit the Sun. There are two major groups of planets in the solar system. Mercury, Venus, Earth, and Mars are **terrestrial planets.** They are close to the Sun, small, and made of rock. Mercury and Venus have no satellites. Earth has one moon, and Mars has two.

Jupiter, Saturn, Uranus, and Neptune are **gas giants.** The gas giants are far from the Sun, huge, and made of gas. Nothing can land on the surface of a gas giant. They all have rings surrounding them, but Saturn's rings are the easiest to see. All the gas giants have moons. Jupiter, the largest of the solar-system planets, has the most moons, 63. Neptune has the fewest, 13.

Pluto is a small, icy body beyond the orbits of the gas giants. It is in a region of icy debris called the **Kuiper Belt.** Pluto is smaller than Earth's **Moon.**

Other Solar-System Objects

The small terrestrial planets are separated from the gas giants by the asteroid belt. This is a collection of millions of rocky chunks orbiting the Sun. Occasionally one gets knocked out of orbit. Some of the most interesting solar-system objects are comets. They come from the Kuiper Belt or even farther out. Comets have large oval orbits that only rarely bring them into the inner solar system. Some comets come back close to the Sun after a million years.

Everything Goes Around

Moving objects travel in straight lines unless a force acts to change their direction. Planets are moving objects. They should travel in straight lines and fly out of the solar system. But the planets don't fly off into space because Sun's **gravity** pulls on the planets and changes their direction of travel. The result is almost-circular orbits around the Sun.

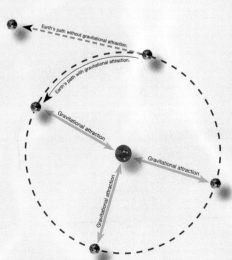

Planets of the Solar System

Mercury

Venus

Earth

Mars

Relative sizes of planets

Jupiter

Saturn

Uranus

Saturn

Pluto
(dwarf planet)

Neptune

Summary Questions

Now is a good time to review what you have recorded in your science notebook. Think about the solar system and the objects that are found in it.

1. What are the main objects in the solar system? How are they alike or different?

2. What is the Sun? What is it made of? What is its role in the solar system?

3. Why do the planets and other objects in the solar system stay in their orbits?

California Science Standards

ES5a. Students know the Sun, an average star, is the central and largest body in the solar system and is composed primarily of hydrogen and helium.

ES5b. Students know the solar system includes the planet Earth, the Moon, the Sun, eight other planets and their satellites, and smaller objects, such as asteroids and comets.

ES5c. Students know the path of a planet around the Sun is due to the gravitational attraction between the Sun and the planet.

Vocabulary

Milky Way

star

Sun

planet

satellite

asteroid

comet

orbit

solar system

Earth

hydrogen

helium

terrestrial planet

gas giant

Kuiper Belt

Moon

gravity

Extensions

Math Problem of the Week

Jaine, who is 10, is curious about how old she would be on other planets in the solar system. She knows that on Earth a year equals 365 days. But other planets have longer or shorter years. How can she figure out how old she would be on these planets?

1. How many Earth days old is Jaine?

2. How many Mercury years old is Jaine?

3. How many Mars years old is Jaine?

4. On which planets is Jaine less than a year old?

5. On which planets is Jaine older than she is on Earth?

PLANET	ORBIT IN EARTH DAYS
Mercury	88
Venus	225
Mars	687
Jupiter	4,333
Saturn	10,759
Uranus	30,685
Neptune	60,189
Pluto (dwarf planet)	90,465

Home/School Connection

What solar-system objects can you see in the night sky? Only one star is a solar-system object, our Sun. But it can't be seen in the night sky.

Four solar-system objects can be seen easily with your bare eyes at night. They are the Moon, Venus, Mars, and Jupiter. They are brighter than the stars. But you have to know when and where to look for them. They aren't visible all night, every night.

Two more planets can be seen with bare eyes if you know where to look, Mercury and Saturn. They are only as bright as stars.

Look for solar-system time and place information in the newspaper or on the Internet. Stardate is a good site. Go to www.stardate.org and then go to stargazing/planet viewing. See how many solar-system objects you can find in the night sky.

I&E6d. Identify the dependent and controlled variables in an investigation.

I&E6e. Identify a single independent variable in a scientific investigation and explain how this variable can be used to collect information to answer a question about the results of the experiment.

Galileo

Galileo Galilei (1564–1642) changed the science of astronomy. He was the first to use a telescope to look into the solar system. Galileo described features of Mars, Jupiter, and Saturn. He made the first maps of the Moon's surface, and discovered satellites orbiting Jupiter. But Galileo made other important scientific discoveries, too.

The lamp that Galileo observed in the cathedral at Pisa, Italy

The first scientific observations of **pendulums** were made by Galileo. His interest in pendulums started in church. Galileo was watching a lamp swinging from the ceiling of the cathedral at Pisa in Italy. The slow back-and-forth motion seemed steady. Galileo used his pulse to time how long it took the lamp to complete one **cycle.**

Galileo continued to watch the lamp. The distance it traveled got shorter and shorter. But the time required to complete a cycle remained the same! How could that be? The lamp always took the same length of time to complete a cycle.

In 1602 Galileo began conducting experiments. He wanted to find out if a pendulum's **period** was really always the same. A period is the length of time it takes a pendulum to complete a cycle. Galileo changed the length of the pendulum. He changed the release position. He changed the mass of the **bob.**

After hundreds of experiments, Galileo understood how pendulums work. It didn't matter how high he lifted the bob before releasing it. And it didn't matter how heavy the bob was. The period was always the same. But when he made the pendulum shorter, the period was shorter. And when he made the pendulum longer, the period was longer. The length of the pendulum was related to the period of swinging.

The First Modern Scientist

Many people who study the history of science agree that Galileo was the first modern scientist. Galileo believed that the only way to find out how things work was to do experiments and make careful observations. He may have been first to conduct **controlled experiments.** What does it mean to do a controlled experiment?

Anything you can change in an experiment that might affect the outcome is called a **variable.** Galileo wondered if the variable of release position affected the period of the pendulum. To find out, he designed a controlled experiment.

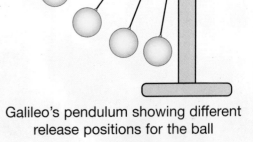

Galileo's pendulum is shown on the right. The system has a ball hanging on a string. The ball can be released from many different positions, as shown. Because Galileo decided on several different release positions before starting the experiment, release position was the **independent variable** in his experiment.

Galileo's pendulum showing different release positions for the ball

To be sure that his results were accurate, Galileo controlled his experiment. He knew that the mass of the pendulum bob might affect the period. He knew the length of the string might affect the period. In order to keep these variables from affecting the period, he kept them exactly the same for every release-position experiment. Mass and length were **controlled variables.**

Galileo then conducted his controlled experiment. Remember, Galileo was doing the experiment to see if release position affects the length of the period. The length of the period might change, so it is a variable. It is called the **dependent variable.** The dependent variable is what you find out as a result of doing the experiment.

Variables Review

There are three kinds of variables in a controlled experiment. You used all three kinds when you conducted your experiment to find out if the length of a pendulum affects the number of swings in 15 seconds.

- The independent variable is the one you change. You changed the length of the swinger string in your experiment. You knew the lengths of the new strings before the experiment started. String length was the independent variable.

- The dependent variable is what you find out by doing the experiment. You counted swings for 15 seconds. The number of swings in 15 seconds was the dependent variable.

- All the other variables are the controlled variables. They are the variables that are not allowed to change. You controlled the variables of mass of the bob, release position, and length of time.

Review Questions

1. **What is a variable?**

2. **Galileo conducted controlled experiments to find out if the mass of the pendulum bob affected the period of the swing. Write a description of how he might design his experiment.**

3. **Identify the independent, dependent, and controlled variables in the mass experiment you described in question 2 above.**

I&E6d. Identify the dependent and controlled variables in an investigation.

I&E6g. Record data by using appropriate graphic representations (including charts, graphs, and labeled diagrams) and make inferences based on those data.

Graphing Data

Tina is making a game. This is her idea. The player rolls a steel ball down a ramp. The ball hits a lever, which swings a paddle. The paddle hits a plastic egg and launches it. The egg lands in a basket. Here's the system she is using.

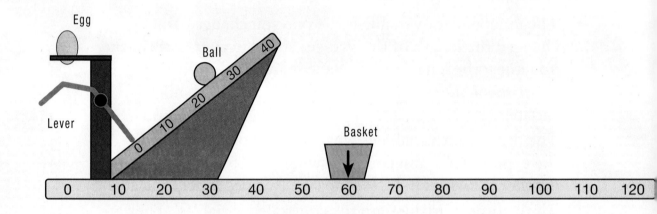

When the ball hits the lever, the paddle sends the egg flying.

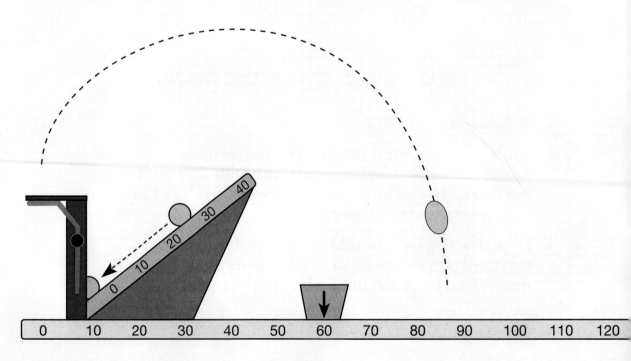

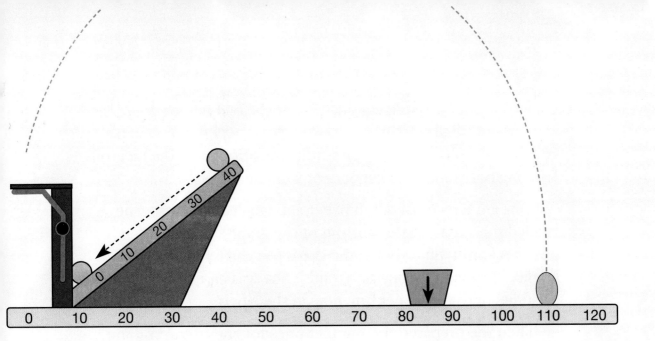

The goal of Tina's game is to catch the egg in the basket. If she can figure out the relationship between the starting point for the ball and the landing place for the egg, she will be able to **predict** how far the egg will fly. Then she will know where to place the basket.

Ball starting position (cm)	Egg landing position (cm)
5	15
10	26
20	55
30	83
40	110

Tina did some experiments. She placed the steel ball at the 40-centimeter (cm) mark on the ramp and let it roll. The egg flew through the air and landed at the 110-cm mark. She recorded these **data.** Then she repeated the experiment four more times, starting the ball at a different place on the ramp each time. When she was done, she organized her data in a T-table.

Making a Two-Coordinate Graph

A **two-coordinate graph** is a plot of the independent variable on the **x-axis** and the dependent variable on the **y-axis.** Tina's two variables are the starting position of the steel ball and the landing position of the egg. But which variable is independent and which is dependent?

The independent variable is the one you know before the experiment starts. Does Tina know the starting position of the ball or the landing position of the egg?

Tina knows the starting position of the ball before doing the experiment. Ball starting position is the independent variable (x-axis). She observes the egg landing position after the ball rolls. Landing position is the dependent variable (y-axis).

Tina got a piece of graph paper and labeled the axes. She labeled the x-axis (at the bottom of the graph) "Ball starting position (cm)." She labeled the y-axis (on the left side of the graph) "Egg landing position (cm)." She was careful to include the units of distance, centimeters, in the labels.

Then she prepared the number lines for the two axes. She looked at her data table to find the highest value for each variable. The number line for the x-axis had to go from 0 to 40. She decided each line on the x-axis would be 2.5 cm. The number line for the y-axis had to go from 0 to 110. Each line on the y-axis would be 5 cm. The graph was set up.

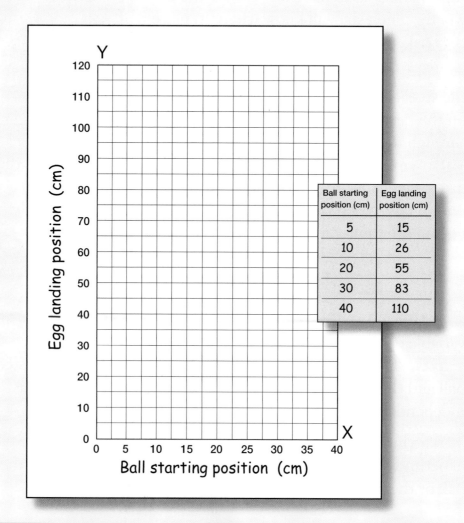

Ball starting position (cm)	Egg landing position (cm)
5	15
10	26
20	55
30	83
40	110

Tina plotted the data pairs. The first pair was (5, 15). She found five on the x-axis, ran her finger up the 5 line until she came to the 15 line on the y-axis. She made a dot at that point. Then she plotted the other four data pairs.

When she had the five points plotted, she drew a best-fit line that showed a relationship. The graph made it clear. The farther up the ramp the ball started, the farther the egg flew.

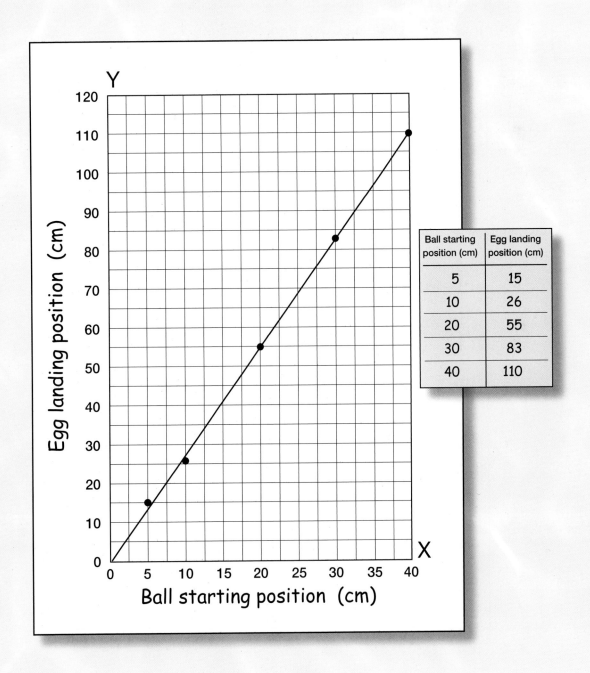

Ball starting position (cm)	Egg landing position (cm)
5	15
10	26
20	55
30	83
40	110

Now back to the game. Tina made a set of 40 cards. She wrote the numbers from 1 to 40 on the cards. The starting position of the ball is determined by drawing a card.

The first time Tina plays the game she draws card number 22. Where should she place the basket to catch the egg? To find out, she uses her graph to predict how far the egg will fly. She finds 22 on the x-axis, follows it up to the graph line, and follows across to the y-axis. The graph tells her to place the basket at 60 cm.

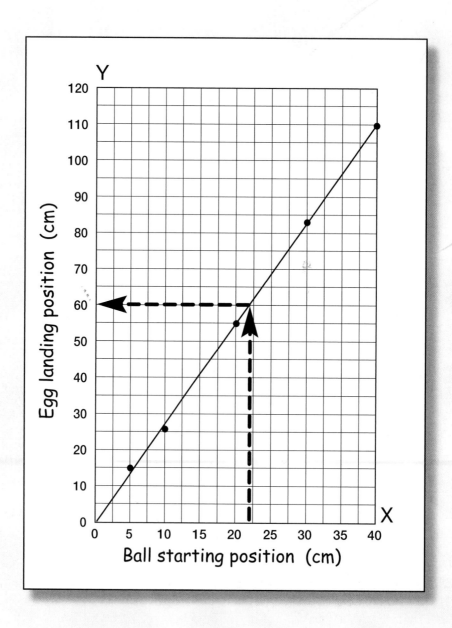

Tina places the basket at 60 cm and releases the ball at 22 cm. The ball rolls, the egg flies, and it lands in the basket. Success! The graph makes it possible for Tina to predict accurately where the egg will land.

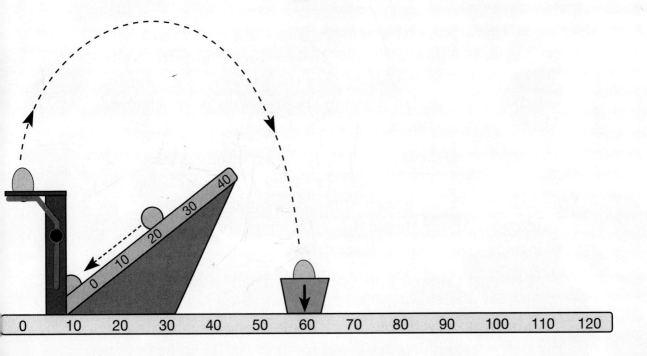

Review Questions

1. **What is the difference between the independent variable and the dependent variable in an experiment?**

2. **Which variable is placed on the x-axis?**

3. **Which variable is placed on the y-axis?**

4. **Which variables did Tina control in her experiments?**

5. **Tina drew card number 13 in her next game. Where should she place the basket to catch the egg?**

6. **In the next game, Tina placed the basket at the 68-cm position and caught the egg. What number did she draw?**

Summary: Swingers

Galileo gazed at a swinging lamp and wondered why it moved the way it did. It went back and forth, each swing a little shorter than the one before it. But the length of time needed to complete one swing never changed. The period was constant.

Galileo thought about all the things that might affect the swinging of the lamp. Could the mass of the bob change the period? Maybe the length of the rope holding the lamp made a difference. All the things that can change that might affect the swinging of the lamp are **variables.**

A swinging lamp is one example of a pendulum. In his lab, Galileo set up a standard pendulum and observed its period. That is, he observed how long it took the pendulum to swing through one complete back-and-forth cycle. Then he designed **controlled experiments** to find out how the variables affected the period. In a controlled experiment, only one variable can change. All the other variables must be kept the same.

Galileo wanted to find out if release position affected the period. He conducted a series of experiments in which he raised the pendulum bob a little higher each time before releasing it. In this experiment, release position is the **independent variable.** Galileo observed, measured, and recorded the exact release position *before* he released the pendulum.

In this experiment, the period is the **dependent variable.** The dependent variable is what you observe, measure, and record as a result of doing the experiment. The dependent variable is what you find out.

All the other variables are **controlled variables.** Controlled variables are not allowed to change. They are not observed, measured, or recorded. Only the independent and dependent variables are recorded.

By conducting controlled experiments, Galileo figured out that the length of a pendulum is directly related to its period. Longer pendulums have longer periods. But is there a pattern to the relationship? The quickest way to find out is to gather experimental **data** and make a **two-coordinate graph.**

Two-Coordinate Graphs

You did an experiment similar to those done by Galileo. But instead of measuring the period of the pendulum, you counted the number of cycles (periods) in 15 seconds. Then you made a graph. The labeled graph below is set up in the proper way. You should follow these rules when making graphs of your own.

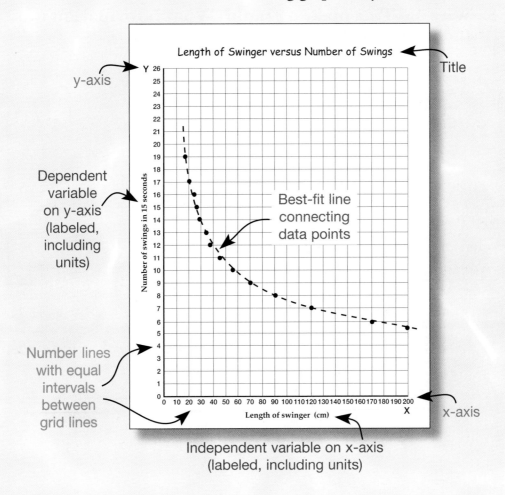

179

A two-coordinate graph can be used to make predictions. If you know the length of a swinger, you can use the graph on page 179 to **predict** how many times the swinger will swing in 15 seconds. And you may remember that Tina used her graph to predict where to position the basket to catch the flying egg in her game. You will find many uses for graphs as you continue your science studies.

Summary Questions

Now is a good time to review what you have recorded in your science notebook. Think about the investigations you have conducted with swingers.

1. **What variables did Galileo test when he conducted his pendulum experiments?**

2. **Galileo conducted experiments to see if length affects the period of a pendulum. What was the independent variable in his experiments? What was the dependent variable? What variables did he control?**

3. **Why did Tina make a graph? What information was she able to get from her graph?**

California Science Standards

I&E6d. Identify the dependent and controlled variables in an investigation.
I&E6e. Identify a single independent variable in a scientific investigation and explain how this variable can be used to collect information to answer a question about the results of the experiment.
I&E6g. Record data by using appropriate graphic representations (including charts, graphs, and labeled diagrams) and make inferences based on those data.

Vocabulary

variable
controlled experiment
independent variable
dependent variable
controlled variable
data
two-coordinate graph
predict

Extensions

Math Problem of the Week

Eight students made swingers of different lengths. Their teacher asked them to find out how many times their pendulum would swing. What the teacher forgot to tell the students was how long to count the swings. These are the data collected by students. From this information, can you put the pendulums in order from shortest to longest?

Student	Number of swings	Length of time (sec.)
1	9	20
2	11	12
3	9	15
4	36	30
5	10	10
6	10	15
7	8	20
8	10	12

Home/School Connection

There was a time when pendulums played an important role in everyday life as time regulators. The predictable swinging of the pendulum was linked to the hands of a clock. Now pendulum clocks are historical curiosities for the most part. Some clock fanciers still have a cuckoo clock, school clock, or grandfather clock as a reminder of a time past.

Make a Second Timer

You can make a second timer at home with a mass, like a fishing weight or a big washer, and some string or thread. Try to get it as accurate as possible. Fine-tune it until you can call 15 seconds at the same time another family member sees the second hand on a clock hit 15 seconds.

Ride the Pendulum

What's a playground swing but a big pendulum you can ride? Can you guess how many cycles (complete swings back and forth) a swing will make in 30 seconds? Will longer swings complete more or fewer cycles in 30 seconds? Take a ride and find out.

ES3b. Students know when liquid water evaporates, it turns into water vapor in the air and can reappear as a liquid when cooled or as a solid if cooled below the freezing point of water.

Drying Up

You know when something is wet. It is covered with water, or it has soaked up a lot of water. When it rains, everything outside gets wet. When you go swimming, you and your swimsuit get wet. Clothes are wet when they come out of the washer, and a dog is wet after a bath.

But things don't stay wet forever. Things get dry, often by themselves. An hour or two after the rain stops, porches, sidewalks, and plants are dry. After a break from swimming to eat lunch, you and your swimsuit are dry. After a few hours on the clothesline, clothes are dry. A dog is dry and fluffy after a short time. Where does the water go?

The water **evaporates.** When water evaporates, it changes from water in its **liquid** form to water in its **gas** form. The gas form of water is called **water vapor.** The water vapor leaves the wet object and goes into the **air.** As the water evaporates, the wet object gets dry.

What happens when you put a wet object in a sealed container? It stays wet. If you put your wet swimsuit in a plastic bag, it's still wet when you take it out of the bag. Why? A little bit of the water in your suit evaporates, but it can't escape into the air. The water vapor has no place to go, so your suit is still wet when you get home.

Have you ever seen water vapor in the air? No, water vapor is invisible. When water changes into vapor, it changes into individual **water molecules.** Water molecules are too small to be seen. The water molecules move into the air among the nitrogen and oxygen molecules. Water vapor becomes part of the air. When water becomes part of the air, it is no longer liquid water.

Review Questions

1. **What is water vapor?**
2. **Where is water vapor?**
3. **What does water vapor look like?**
4. **What happens when a wet object gets dry?**

INVESTIGATION 3

ES3b. Students know when liquid water evaporates, it turns into water vapor in the air and can reappear as a liquid when cooled or as a solid if cooled below the freezing point of water.

Evaporation

Evaporation is the change from liquid to gas. In the case of water, liquid water changes into water vapor. The water vapor then moves into the air. But what actually happens when evaporation takes place? To find out, we have to think about water as molecules.

A water molecule is made of three **atoms,** two hydrogen atoms and one oxygen atom. Scientists have figured out that one water molecule looks like this.

A representation of one water molecule

When water is in its liquid state, the molecules are all attracted to one another and in contact with each other. But they are not attached together tightly. As a result, the molecules move around and over one another. The molecules are in constant motion. That is why liquid water flows.

If you could see the molecules in a tiny spot of liquid water, they would look something like this.

A representation of many water molecules

Remember, the molecules are in constant motion. They are bumping into each other all the time. Sometimes a water molecule at the surface gets bumped so hard that it is knocked free from the mass of liquid. The free molecule moves into the air as a water-vapor molecule.

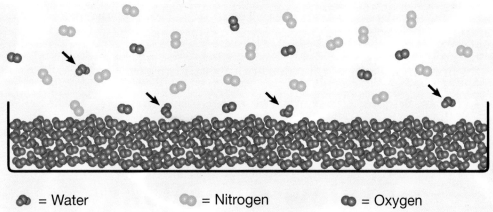

= Water   = Nitrogen   = Oxygen

Water molecules go into the air, which is mostly nitrogen and oxygen molecules.

Adding Heat

The rate at which water molecules escape from the liquid depends on how hard the water molecules hit each other. One way to increase the force with which molecules hit each other is to heat them up. When water is heated, the molecules move faster. When fast-moving molecules hit each other, they hit each other harder. As a result, more molecules break free from the surface of hot water than from cold water.

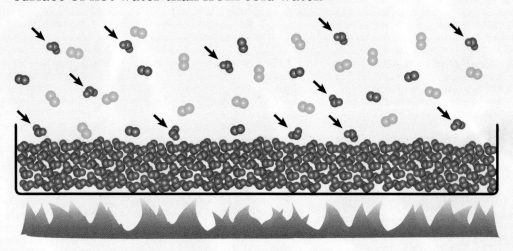

Water evaporates faster when water is heated.

There is a limit to the amount of water vapor that can enter the air. When the air has taken in as much water vapor as it can, the air is **saturated** with water vapor. Cold air can hold only a small amount of water vapor. It doesn't take much evaporated water to saturate cold air.

Warm air is different. Warm air can take in a lot of water vapor before it is saturated. But there is still a limit to the amount of water vapor that warm air can hold.

There are two general rules about evaporation.

1. The warmer the water, the faster it evaporates.

2. The warmer the air, the more water vapor it can hold.

Review Questions

1. **What causes evaporation?**

2. **Why does warm water evaporate faster than cold water?**

3. **How is water vapor different from liquid water?**

4. **How does temperature affect the amount of water vapor in the air?**

ES3b. Students know when liquid water evaporates, it turns into water vapor in the air and can reappear as a liquid when cooled or as a solid if cooled below the freezing point of water.

Surface-Area Experiment

Julie and Art wanted to find out how **surface area** affects evaporation. They decided to do an experiment. They had some plastic boxes to put water in, some graph paper, and a set of measuring tools. They were ready to start.

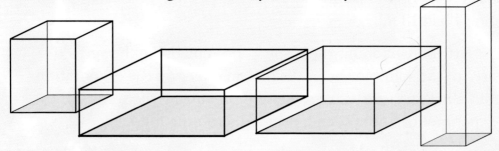

Julie had an idea for measuring the surface area of each box. She traced around each box on the graph paper. She used the meter tape to measure the distance between the lines on the graph paper. The lines were 1 centimeter (cm) apart.

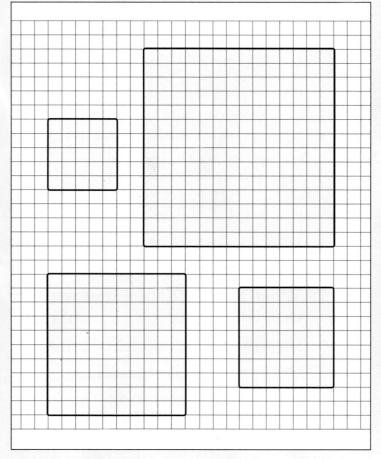

The two students numbered the boxes. The box with the smallest surface area was number 1. Then they measured 50 milliliters (ml) of water into each box. They placed the four boxes on the counter by a window.

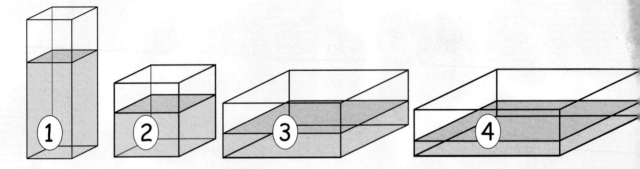

One week later Julie and Art measured the amount of water in each box. Box 1 had 46 ml. Box 2 had 42 ml. Box 3 had 34 ml. Box 4 had 18 ml.

Art thought about the results. It seemed like the surface area of the water in the boxes had an effect on the evaporation. But he wasn't sure. Julie suggested organizing the results of the experiment. The students decided to do the following.

- Make a T-table to display their data.

- Make a graph of their data.

- Describe what they learned from the experiment.

Can you help Julie and Art? Use the information they gathered to write a report about the effect of surface area on evaporation. Be sure to include the three kinds of information listed above.

Review Questions

1. **What was the independent variable in Julie and Art's experiment?**

2. **What was the dependent variable in their experiment?**

3. **What variables did they control?**

4. **What additional information would be useful to better understand how surface area affects evaporation?**

ES3b. Students know when liquid water evaporates, it turns into water vapor in the air and can reappear as a liquid when cooled or as a solid if cooled below the freezing point of water.

Condensation

When water evaporates, where does it go? It goes into the air. Water is always evaporating. Clothes are drying on clotheslines. Wet streets are drying after a rain. Water is evaporating from lakes and oceans all the time. Every day more than 1,000 cubic kilometers (km^3) of water evaporates worldwide. And all that water vapor goes into the air! That's nearly 240 cubic miles of water. That amount of water would cover the entire state of California 3 meters (10 feet) deep.

What happens to all that water in the air? As long as the air stays warm, the water stays in the air as water vapor. Warmth (heat) is energy. As long as the molecules of water vapor have a lot of energy in the form of heat, they continue to exist as gas.

But if the air cools, things change. As the air cools, all the molecules lose energy and slow down. This is when molecules of water vapor start to come together. Slowing down and coming together is called **condensation.** Condensation is the change from gas to liquid.

Molecules of condensed water vapor form tiny masses of liquid water. When invisible water vapor in the atmosphere condenses, the water becomes visible again. **Clouds** and **fog** are made of these tiniest masses of liquid water.

Condensation usually happens on a cold surface. In class you observed condensation on the cold surface of a plastic cup filled with ice water. But there are no cups of ice water in the sky. What kind of surface does water vapor condense on?

Most condensation in the air starts with dust particles. Water molecules attach to a dust particle. When a tiny mass of water has formed on a dust particle, other water molecules will join the liquid mass.

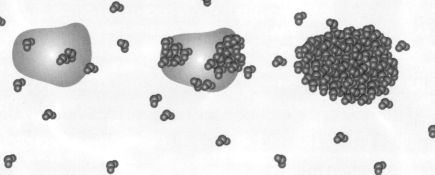

The mass grows and grows until a tiny droplet of water has formed.

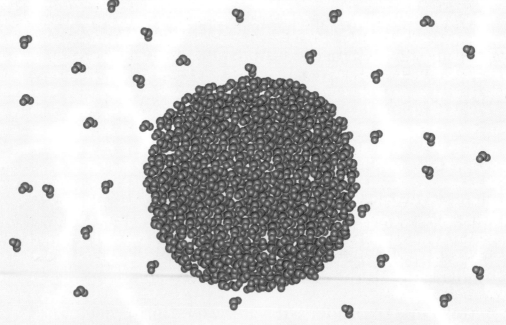

When you look up in the sky and see clouds, you are seeing droplets of liquid water. Each droplet is made up of billions of water molecules, but a single droplet is still too small to see. But you can see them when trillions and trillions of them are close together in clouds.

Where else have you seen condensation besides up in the sky in the form of clouds? Sometimes water vapor condenses close to the ground. This is called fog. Being in fog is really being in a cloud that is at ground level.

Fog close to the ground

As you know, water vapor doesn't always condense in air. If you go out early in the morning following a warm day, you might see condensation called **dew.** In the pictures below, dew formed on a spider web and along the edges of the leaves on a plant.

Dew on a spider web

Dew on plant leaves

Condensation on a window

Water vapor condenses indoors, too. On a cold morning you might see condensation on your kitchen window. Or if you go outside into the cold wearing your glasses, they could get fogged with condensation when you go back inside.

What happens to the bathroom mirror after you take a shower? The air in the bathroom is warm and saturated with water vapor. When the air makes contact with the cool mirror, the water vapor condenses on the smooth surface. That's why the mirror is foggy and wet.

Condensation on glasses

Condensation on the mirror

When the temperature drops below the **freezing point** of water (0°C or 32°F), water vapor will condense and freeze. Frozen condensation is called **frost**. Frost is tiny crystals of ice. Frost might form on a car window on a cold night. You can also see frost on plants early on a winter morning. But you have to get up before the Sun if you want to see the beautiful frost patterns.

Frost on a window

Frost on plants

Review Questions

1. **What is condensation?**

2. **What role does temperature play in condensation?**

3. **What is frost?**

4. **Why does condensation form on a glass of iced tea?**

Summary: Water Vapor

ater is a unique substance. It exists on Earth in all three common states of matter, solid, liquid, and gas. The solid state is called ice. The liquid state is called liquid water, or just water. The gas state is called **water vapor.**

Water changes between the gas and liquid states easily. When liquid water changes to water vapor, we say the water dried up. When we describe the change from liquid to gas scientifically, we say the water **evaporated.**

When liquid water appears out of thin air, we have several common names for it. The name we use depends on when and where the water appears. When it appears as tiny droplets in the air, we call it **clouds** and **fog.** When it appears on windows, plants, and cars, we call it **dew.** The scientific name for water that appears out of the air is **condensation.**

What causes water to evaporate and condense? Energy in the form of heat.

When you put a pan of water on the stove, heat energy transfers to the **water molecules.** The water molecules move faster and bang into one another harder. Molecules at the surface of the water get knocked free. The free molecules enter the air as water vapor. The larger the **surface area** of water exposed to air, the faster the water evaporates.

The mixture of gases we call air is all free molecules. Most of the air molecules are nitrogen and oxygen. Water molecules are a small but important part of the air. Water vapor will never be a large part of the air because there is a limit to the amount of water the air can hold. When air is holding all the water vapor it can, the air is **saturated.**

Warm air can hold more water vapor than cold air. This is a very important idea. Think about a mass of warm air that is saturated with water vapor. What will happen if the mass of warm, saturated air cools down? Cool air can't hold as much water as warm air. What will happen to the water in the air?

When water vapor cools, molecules move slower. Slower water molecules start to stick together. Water molecules in contact with one another condense to form liquid water.

Condensation usually starts on a surface of some kind. It could be a window or a plant. Or it could be a tiny bit of dust floating around in the air. Once a few molecules of water have condensed on a surface, other molecules will condense on the tiny spot of liquid water. The spot of water will grow until it is big enough to see. Visible condensation is known as clouds, fog, and dew.

Fog and low clouds over South San Francisco, California

When the temperature is below freezing (0°C or 32°F), you might see **frost** in the early morning. Frost is frozen condensation. It can form on windows, cars, and outdoor plants. Frost is made of tiny crystals of ice. The patterns created by the crystals in frost can be very beautiful. But to see them you have to get up early. As soon as sunshine falls on the frost, it will melt. If you get up late, all you will see is dew.

Summary Questions

Now is a good time to review what you have recorded in your science notebook. Think about the evaporation and condensation investigations you conducted.

1. **What happens when liquid water evaporates?**

2. **What happens when water vapor condenses?**

3. **What is frost and how does it form?**

California Science Standard

ES3b. Students know when liquid water evaporates, it turns into water vapor in the air and can reappear as a liquid when cooled or as a solid if cooled below the freezing point of water.

Vocabulary

water vapor

evaporate

cloud

fog

dew

condensation

water molecule

surface area

saturate

frost

Extensions

Math Problem of the Week

Some students set up an investigation to find out what effect surface area has on the rate of evaporation. They used a cake pan, a water glass, a cottage-cheese container, and an olive jar. The students put 100 ml of water in each container. They measured the water remaining in each container on days 2, 4, and 6.

Container	Water remaining on		
	Day 2	Day 4	Day 6
Cake pan	75 ml	50 ml	25 ml
Water glass	90 ml	80 ml	70 ml
Cottage-cheese	80 ml	60 ml	40 ml
Olive jar	95 ml	90 ml	85 ml

1. In which container will all the water evaporate first? On which day will that happen?

2. In which container will all the water evaporate last? On which day will that happen?

Home/School Connection

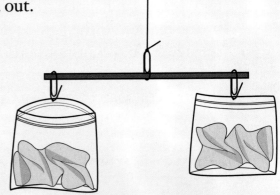

How fast does water evaporate in your home? Set up an evaporation gizmo to find out.

You will need

1   Plastic soda straw

3   Paper clips

1   Piece of string

2   Zip bags, same size

2   Paper towels

Moisten the paper towels. Put one in each bag. Seal one bag and leave the other open. Balance the system. Observe.

Where did the water go? The amount of water vapor in the air is called **humidity.** When air contains as much water vapor as it can possibly hold, the humidity is 100%. How could the humidity of the air affect the rate of evaporation?

ES4a. Students know uneven heating of Earth causes air movements (convection currents).

Uneven Heating

Stars are huge energy generators. Energy shines out from them in all directions. Most of this energy streams out into space and never hits anything. A small amount, however, hits objects in the universe. When you look into the sky on a dark, clear night, you see thousands of stars. You see them because a tiny amount of energy from the stars goes into your eye.

During the day, you are aware of the energy coming from a much closer star, the Sun. The most important forms of energy coming from the Sun are heat and light. When heat and light come to Earth, you can feel the heat and see the light. Heat and light from the Sun are called **solar energy.**

When light from the Sun hits matter, such as Earth's surface, two things can happen. The light can be **reflected** or absorbed by the matter. If the light is reflected, it simply bounces off the matter and continues in a new direction. But if the light is absorbed, the matter gains energy. Usually the added energy is in the form of heat. When matter absorbs energy, its temperature goes up.

Sunset over a bay in Baja California

Heating It Up

The amount of solar energy coming from the Sun is pretty uniform. But the temperature of Earth's surface is not uniform. Some locations get warmer than other locations. Why is that?

There are several variables that affect how hot a material will get when solar energy shines on it. The table below lists several variables and how each affects the temperature change of a material.

Variable	Effect
Length of exposure	Longer exposure = higher temperature
Intensity of solar energy	Greater intensity = higher temperature
Color of material	Darker color = higher temperature
Properties of material	Water shows the least temperature change

Length of exposure is how long the Sun shines on an object.

Intensity of solar energy is how concentrated the energy is. If the light has to shine through clouds, for instance, the intensity will be reduced. Clouds reflect and absorb some of the energy before it gets to Earth's surface. The brighter the sunshine falling on an object, the warmer the object will be.

Color is important because different colors absorb solar energy differently. Black absorbs the most solar energy. White absorbs the least solar energy.

The chemical properties of materials affect how hot they get when they absorb solar energy. As you found out in your experiments, a volume of soil gets a lot hotter than an equal volume of water when they are put side by side in the sunshine. Water heats up slowly and soil heats up rapidly when they get the same amount of energy. Water cools slowly and soil cools rapidly when they are moved to the shade.

Solar Energy in Action

Think about a summer trip to the beach. On a cloudless day the Sun shines down with equal intensity on the town of San Clemente, the sandy beach, and the ocean. It's a hot day.

When the car stops in the parking lot in the early afternoon, the parking lot is hot. The black asphalt has absorbed a lot of solar energy, and its temperature is 50°C (120°F)! You are anxious to get to the beach. You dash across the hot parking lot and onto the white sand. Whew! The white sand isn't as hot. It is a bearable 32°C (90°F). You keep going, right into the water. You finally get relief from the intense southern California heat. The temperature of the ocean water is 22°C (72°F).

The asphalt, sand, and seawater were all subjected to the same intensity of solar energy for the same length of time. But they are all different temperatures.

Black asphalt absorbs a lot of energy and gets very hot. White sand reflects a lot of solar energy. Sand doesn't get as hot as asphalt. Water absorbs a lot of energy, but it stays cool.

The temperature of Earth's surface is not the same everywhere. Land gets hotter than water in the sunshine. Land gets colder than water when the Sun goes down. Land heats up and cools off rapidly. Water heats up and cools off slowly. The result is **uneven heating** of Earth's surface.

Uneven Heating Worldwide

You can experience uneven heating of Earth's surface with your bare feet during a trip to the beach. The difference in temperature between the asphalt and water is obvious. On a larger scale, the whole planet is heated unevenly. The tropics (near the equator) are warmer. The polar areas are cooler. That's because the intensity of the solar energy is greater in the tropics.

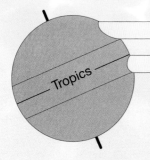

A beam of sunlight spreads over a larger area toward the poles.

The illustration shows how sunshine comes straight down on the tropics. But the sunshine comes at an angle toward the poles. You can see how the same amount of light is spread over a much larger area in the north than in the tropics. This results in uneven heating between the tropics and the polar areas.

Review Questions

1. **What causes Earth's surface to heat up?**

2. **What are some of the variables that cause uneven heating of Earth's surface?**

3. **What happens to the temperature of equal volumes of soil and water when they are placed in the sunshine for 30 minutes?**

INVESTIGATION 4

ES4a. Students know uneven heating of Earth causes air movements (convection currents).

Wind!

Kite flying can be a lot of fun if the conditions are right. If the conditions are wrong, kite flying can be a drag. What makes conditions right for kite flying? **Wind.**

Wind is air in motion. Air is matter. Air has mass and takes up space. When a mass of air is in motion, it can move things around. Wind can blow leaves down the street, lift your hat off your head, and carry a kite into the air.

Sometimes air is still. Other times the wind is blowing. What causes the wind to blow? What puts the air into motion? The answer is energy. It takes energy to move air. The energy to create wind comes from the Sun.

Wind lifts a kite into the air.

Air is molecules of oxygen and nitrogen (and a few other gases). The molecules are flying around and banging into each other, the land, and the sea. Let's imagine we are back at the beach at San Clemente. It's early morning. The air over the land and the air over the sea are both the same cool temperature.

Air (molecules)

Sea

Land

In early morning, the land, sea, and air are all the same cool temperature.

As the Sun shines down on the land and sea, solar energy is absorbed. The land heats up quickly. The sea heats up very slowly. By noon the land is hot, but the sea is still cool. Earth's surface is heated unevenly. The afternoon wind starts. Here's why.

When air molecules bang into the hot surface of the land, energy transfers to the air molecules. Because of this **energy transfer,** the air molecules fly around faster. The air gets hot. The hot-air molecules bang into each other harder. That pushes the molecules farther apart.

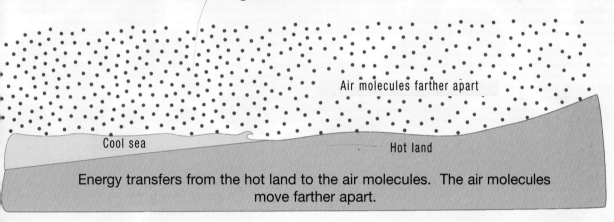

Energy transfers from the hot land to the air molecules. The air molecules move farther apart.

Over the ocean, air molecules are banging into the cool surface of the water. The air stays cool. The air molecules continue to move at a slower speed. The cool-air molecules don't hit each other as hard, so they stay closer together.

A cubic meter of hot air has fewer molecules than a cubic meter of cool air. The hot air is less dense than an equal volume of cool air.

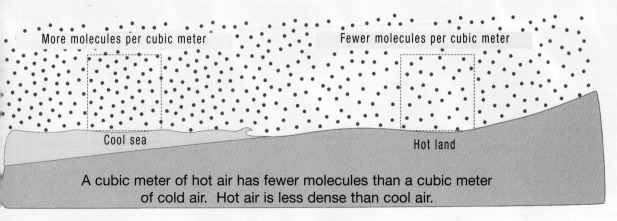

A cubic meter of hot air has fewer molecules than a cubic meter of cold air. Hot air is less dense than cool air.

The Wind Starts

You know that cork floats on water. Cork floats on water because it is less dense than water. If you take a cork to the bottom of the sea and let it go, it will float to the surface.

That's exactly what happens with warm and cold air. The warm air over the land floats upward because it is less dense than the cool air over the sea. The denser, cool air flows into the area where the light, warm air is and pushes it upward. The movement of denser air from the sea to the warm land is wind. Wind is the movement of denser air to an area where the air is less dense.

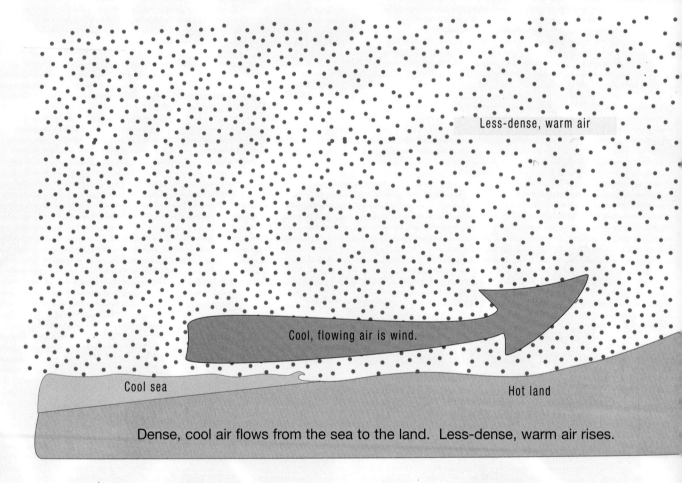

Less-dense, warm air

Cool, flowing air is wind.

Cool sea

Hot land

Dense, cool air flows from the sea to the land. Less-dense, warm air rises.

There is more to the story of wind. Two things happen at the same time to create wind. The warm air cools as it rises, becoming denser than the surrounding air. At the same time, the dense air from the sea warms up as it flows over the hot land.

As a result, air starts to move in a big circle. Air that is warmed by the hot land moves upward. The warm air cools as it moves up, gets denser, and starts to fall. The rising and falling air sets up a big circular air current. The circular current is called a **convection current.**

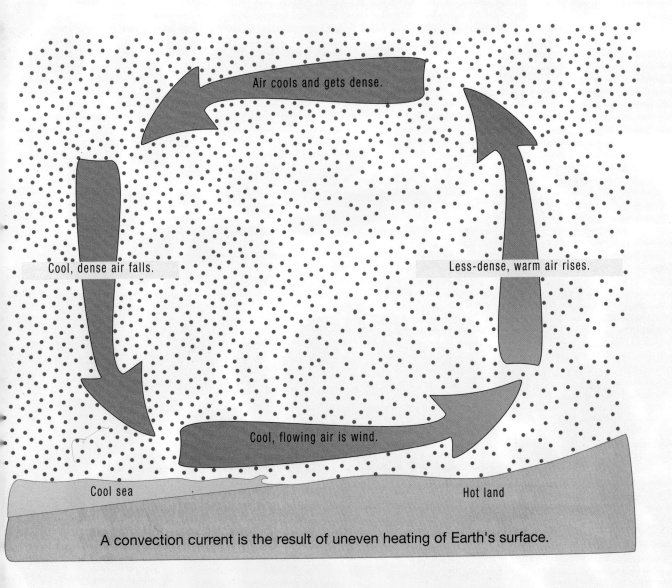

Air cools and gets dense.

Cool, dense air falls.

Less-dense, warm air rises.

Cool, flowing air is wind.

Cool sea

Hot land

A convection current is the result of uneven heating of Earth's surface.

As long as Earth's surface continues to be heated unevenly, the convection current will continue to flow. The part of the convection current that flows across Earth's surface is what we experience as wind. But what happens at night?

The Wind Changes Direction

When the Sun goes down, solar energy no longer falls on the land and sea. The land cools rapidly, but the sea stays at about the same temperature. The air over the cool land is no longer heated. The density of the air over land and sea is the same. The convection current stops flowing. The wind stops blowing.

What will happen if the night is really cold? The land will get cold. The air over the land will get cold. The cold air will become denser than the air over the sea. The denser air will flow from the land to the sea. The convection current will flow in the opposite direction, and the wind will blow from the land to the sea.

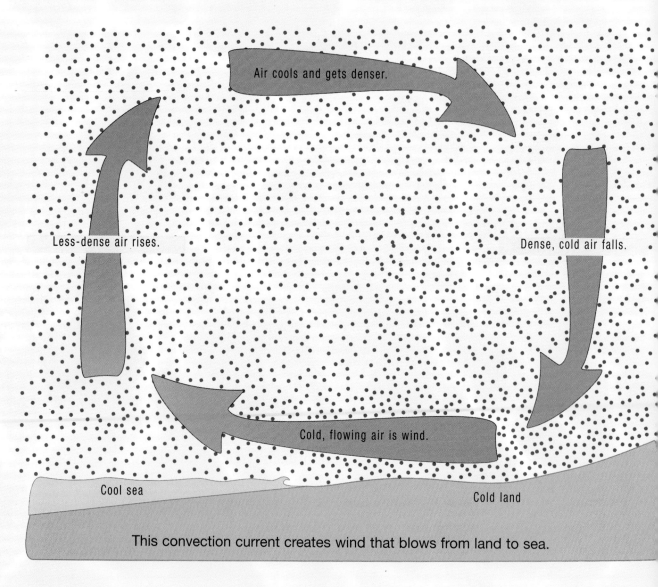

Air cools and gets denser.

Less-dense air rises.

Dense, cold air falls.

Cold, flowing air is wind.

Cool sea

Cold land

This convection current creates wind that blows from land to sea.

Convection Summary

Uneven heating of Earth's surface by the Sun causes uneven heating of the air over Earth's surface. Warm air is less dense than cold air. Cold, dense air flows to an area where the air is warmer and less dense. The less-dense air is pushed upward. As the warm air moves upward, it cools. Cool air is denser, so it falls back to Earth. This circular pattern of air flow is a convection current.

Convection currents produce wind. The greater the difference in temperature between the warm and cold air masses, the harder and faster the wind will blow. Uneven heating of Earth's surface is the cause of many weather changes on Earth, including hurricanes, tornadoes, and thunderstorms.

Review Questions

1. **Explain how convection currents are produced in the air.**

2. **Explain what causes wind.**

3. **Describe what happens to air molecules when air is heated.**

4. **What is the source of energy that causes the wind to blow?**

ES4e. Students know that the Earth's atmosphere exerts a pressure that decreases with distance above Earth's surface and that at any point it exerts this pressure equally in all directions.

The Pressure Is On!

Earth is surrounded by air. The air reaches up about 500 kilometers (300 miles) above Earth's surface. The whole layer of air covering the Earth is the **atmosphere.**

Air has mass. How much? Imagine putting a 1-cm square of paper on the ground. Then think about a column of air 1 centimeter square from the ground all the way up to the top of the atmosphere. The mass of the air resting on that piece of paper would be about 1.2 kilograms (2.6 pounds).

The top of your head has a surface area of about 150 square centimeters. That means every time you stand under the open sky, you have the pressure of 180 kilograms (400 pounds) of air pushing down on the top of your head. That's like wearing a hat with a refrigerator on it! Is it safe to go outdoors?

Don't worry, it's safe. The force caused by the mass of the air above you is called **atmospheric pressure.** Your body can easily push back with a force equal to the atmospheric pressure. You are usually not aware of the pressure at all. But sometimes you are. Have you ever felt your ears "pop"? That sometimes happens when you are riding down a long hill in a car. What causes that?

Atmospheric Pressure

Air is made of molecules. Molecules have mass. If you pile a lot of molecules on top of each other, the load gets heavier and heavier. That's what the atmosphere is, a huge pile of air molecules.

Imagine molecules as big as watermelons. A big melon is pretty heavy. It might have a mass of 10 kilograms. If you place the melon on a scale, the scale will read 10 kg.

Think about a stack of 10 watermelons. The scale would now read 100 kg. The mass on the scale is equal to the sum of the 10 melons.

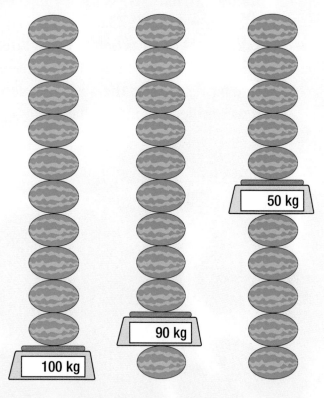

But the pressure is not the same on all the melons. This can be seen by moving the scale from the bottom of the stack of melons to someplace else in the stack. If the scale is moved between melon 1 and melon 2, the mass on the scale is 90 kg. Between melons 5 and 6, the scale reads 50 kg.

Air molecules are tiny, but they stack up the same way. A pressure gauge at Earth's surface will show the pressure that results from a stack of molecules 500 kilometers deep. The pressure is greatest at Earth's surface. This is just like the pressure on the watermelon at the bottom of the stack is greatest.

If you could see air molecules, you would see that they are compressed near Earth's surface. Because the molecules are close together, air is densest near Earth's surface. Denser air has more molecules per unit volume.

Let's imagine that a small vial contains 100 air molecules at Earth's surface.

Vial of 100 air molecules

As you look higher in the atmosphere, you see that the molecules get farther apart. Air higher in the atmosphere is not compressed as much. The air is less dense. The same vial might contain only 50 molecules because the air is less compressed. The molecules are farther apart.

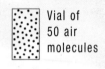
Vial of 50 air molecules

Below is a mountain in the atmosphere. At sea level, the air is dense and the pressure is high. Going up to the top of a tall mountain, like Mt. Whitney in the Sierra Nevada, is like climbing a ladder 4.4 km (2.75 miles) into the air. Up on the mountain, 4.4 kilometers of air is below you. This air is not applying pressure on you. The small mass of air above you does not push with as much pressure, so the air is less dense. That means there are fewer molecules in the vial.

The atmosphere is densest at sea level. The atmosphere gets less and less dense as you rise higher above sea level. As the density of air goes down, so does the atmospheric pressure.

The Effects of Atmospheric Pressure

Atmospheric pressure changes with **elevation.** As you go higher in the atmosphere, the pressure gets lower. Air pushes with less force in the mountains than it does at sea level.

Pressure is a result of air molecules banging into each other and objects. Pressure goes up when *more* molecules are banging into things. This happens when air gets compressed. Pressure goes up when molecules bang into things *harder.* This happens when air gets hot. Because air molecules are flying in all directions, pressure acts in all directions equally.

In class you worked with syringes connected with a tube. When you pulled one plunger out, the other one went in. Why?

Here's a drawing showing two syringes. The density of air molecules inside and outside the syringes is the same.

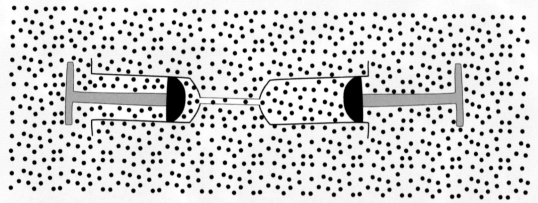

The density of air molecules is the same inside and outside the syringes.

When both plungers are pulled out and held, the number of molecules inside the syringes does not change. But the space they are in gets bigger. The molecules fill the larger space evenly.

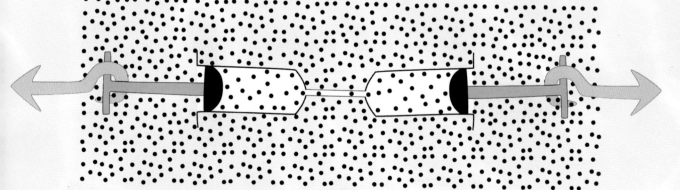

The space inside the two syringes is bigger when the plunger is pulled out. The molecules inside the syringes fill the space, so the density is lower.

211

The density of molecules inside the syringes is lower than the density of molecules outside. That means the air pressure inside the syringes (blue arrows) is lower than the atmospheric pressure outside (red arrows).

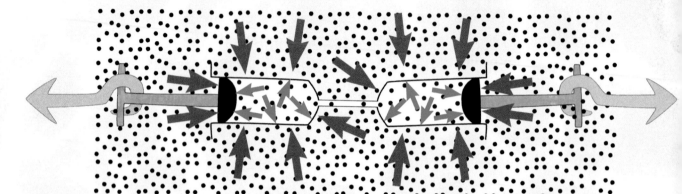

Pressure outside the syringes is greater than pressure inside the syringes.

When the plunger on the right is released, the stronger pressure outside pushes it in until the density of molecules inside the syringes is the same as the density of molecules outside the syringes. When the density is the same, the pressure is the same. The plunger stops moving.

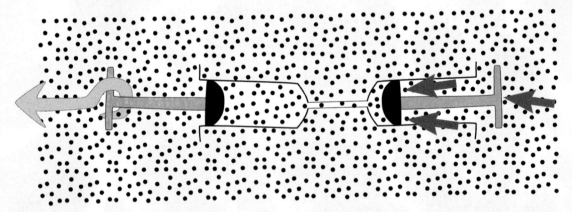

Atmospheric pressure pushes the plunger in until the density of air molecules inside the syringes is equal to the density of molecules outside.

It is important to understand that pulling the plunger out on one syringe does not *suck* the plunger into the other syringe. The right way to think about the event is that pulling out one plunger reduces the pressure inside both syringes. Atmospheric pressure then *pushes* the plunger until the inside and outside pressure are the same.

Atmospheric Pressure and Weather

Meteorologists are scientists who study **weather.** By studying atmospheric pressure, temperature, and humidity, they can predict what the weather will be in a few days or a few weeks. Predicting weather is called **forecasting.**

You have probably heard **weather forecasts** on TV. Often the weather forecasters will mention high pressure or low pressure. They are referring to the atmospheric pressure. Different areas of Earth's surface have slightly different atmospheric temperatures. This can be the result of uneven heating.

Hot air expands, becomes less dense, and exerts less pressure. That makes a local low-pressure area. Cold air contracts, becomes denser, and exerts more pressure. That makes a local high-pressure area. If there is a cooler, high-pressure area near a warm, low-pressure area, the difference in pressure will start a convection current. And that means wind. That's one kind of weather forecast a meteorologist can make.

Review Questions

1. **What is atmospheric pressure and what causes it?**

2. **Is atmospheric pressure higher on a mountaintop or at sea level? Explain why.**

3. **Rudy's family drove from San Francisco to Tioga Pass in Yosemite National Park. The pass is over 3,000 meters high. A bag of chips they had for snacks was puffed up like a pillow when they got to the pass. Why?**

4. **Rudy finished a plastic bottle of spring water on the pass. He put the lid on the empty bottle tightly. When he got back home in San Francisco, the bottle was crushed. Why?**

Summary: Heating Earth

Energy from the Sun in the form of heat and light falls on Earth during the day. Materials on Earth's surface absorb the **solar energy** and get warm. Some materials, such as rock and soil, heat up quickly when they absorb energy. Other materials, such as water, heat up slowly when they absorb energy. The result is **uneven heating** of Earth's surface. The land changes temperature quickly. The oceans change temperature slowly.

Air is a mixture of gas molecules. Most of the molecules are nitrogen and oxygen. Air molecules are flying around all the time. When air molecules bang into Earth's surface, they can gain or lose energy. Gain or loss of energy is **energy transfer.**

On a sunny day, the land gets hot. Air molecules that bang into the land gain energy. Those molecules move faster.

When air molecules bang into a cold surface, such as the ocean, they lose energy. Those molecules move slower.

Molecule Energy and Gas Density

Fast-moving molecules bang into each other harder. When molecules hit hard, they push each other farther apart. When molecules are farther apart, the mass of air is less dense. Slow-moving molecules hit each other with less force. They move closer together. The air becomes denser. As a result of energy transfer, warm air is less dense than cold air.

Convection Currents and Wind

Often uneven heating of Earth's surface results in masses of air of different temperatures. A mass of warm air over the land will be less dense than a mass of cold air over the ocean. When this happens, the cool, dense air will push the warm, less-dense air upward. As the cold air flows onshore, it is warmed by the land. The new warm air is pushed up by more cold air from the sea.

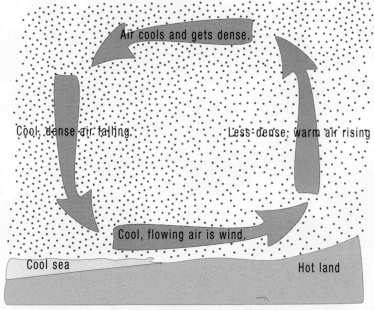

Air cools and gets dense.

Cool, dense air falling.

Less-dense, warm air rising

Cool, flowing air is wind.

Cool sea

Hot land

A convection current is the result of uneven heating of Earth's surface.

As the warm air rises, it cools. When the mass of air cools, it becomes dense and falls back to Earth's surface. The cool, dense air will once again flow onshore.

The circular flow of air is a **convection current.** The part of the convection current where cool air from the sea flows onshore creates **wind.** This is how convection currents produce wind all over Earth.

Atmospheric Pressure

Air molecules have mass. The air molecules stacked up from Earth's surface to the top of the **atmosphere** have a lot of mass. All those molecules push on Earth's surface with a lot of pressure. Because the pressure in the air pushes *in all directions,* air pressure is pushing equally on every side of every object that is in the air.

The pressure exerted by the air is called **atmospheric pressure.** Atmospheric pressure is pushing on all sides of you, as well as your desk, books, school, and town.

Atmospheric pressure is the result of the force applied by the air above you. If you go higher in the atmosphere, to the top of a tall mountain, the atmospheric pressure will be less. When you look down from the mountain, you can see that there is a lot of air below you. That air is not above you, it is below you. Atmospheric pressure is produced by the mass of air above you. Less air above results in less pressure.

The atmosphere is densest at sea level. The atmosphere gets less and less dense as you rise higher above sea level. As the density of air goes down, so does the atmospheric pressure.

When there is less atmospheric pressure, the air molecules are not pushed as close together. The air at the top of a mountain is less dense. When people talk about "thin air," they are really talking about air that is less dense.

Meteorologists are scientists who study **weather.** Differences in atmospheric pressure causes changes in the weather. By measuring the pressure at different places on Earth, meteorologists can make better **weather forecasts.**

Summary Questions

Now is a good time to review what you have recorded in your science notebook. Think about the uneven heating and convection investigations you conducted.

1. **What causes uneven heating of Earth's surface?**

2. **Explain how uneven heating of Earth's surface results in convection currents.**

3. **What is atmospheric pressure and what causes it?**

4. **In what direction does atmospheric pressure push?**

California Science Standards

ES4a. Students know uneven heating of Earth causes air movements (convection currents).

ES4e. Students know that the Earth's atmosphere exerts a pressure that decreases with distance above Earth's surface and that at any point it exerts this pressure equally in all directions.

Vocabulary

solar energy

uneven heating

energy transfer

convection current

wind

atmosphere

atmospheric pressure

meteorologist

weather

weather forecast

Extensions

Math Problem of the Week

Four students had questions about how earth materials heat up in the sunshine.

1. How does length of exposure to sunshine affect final temperature?
2. How does surface area affect the length of time it takes to raise the temperature 10°C?
3. How does the volume of material in the container affect heating?
4. What kind of material heats up fastest in the sunshine?

Each student designed an experiment. The students worked with these variables.

Size of container   Kind of earth material   Volume of material

Color   Time   Temperature

Identify the independent, dependent, and controlled variables in each experiment.

Experiment	Independent variable	Dependent variable	Controlled variables
1	Time	Temperature	Size, kind, volume, color
2			
3			
4			

Home/School Connection

Look at seed packets or seed catalogs to find out how many days it takes for some of your favorite vegetables to bear fruit. Count each day as a "sun day" and compare the results for different plants.

Where Is Earth's Water?

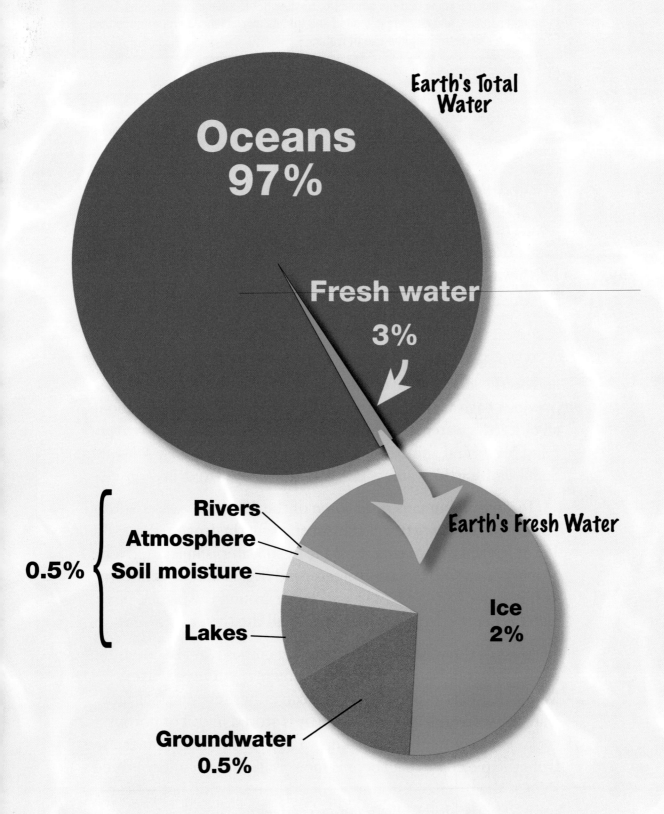

Oceans 97%

Earth's Total Water

Fresh water 3%

Rivers
Atmosphere
0.5% { Soil moisture
Lakes

Earth's Fresh Water

Ice 2%

Groundwater 0.5%

ES3a. Students know most of Earth's water is present as salt water in the oceans, which cover most of Earth's surface.

ES3d. Students know that the amount of fresh water located in rivers, lakes, underground sources, and glaciers is limited and that its availability can be extended by recycling and decreasing the use of water.

Earth's Water

Earth is known as the water planet. Earth is the only planet that has vast oceans of water. Seventy-one percent of Earth's surface is covered by water. If your first view of Earth from space was of the Pacific Ocean, you might think Earth was completely covered in water.

Where Is Earth's Water?

Water is almost everywhere on Earth. It's in the oceans, in and on the land, and in the atmosphere. The pie charts on the previous page show how Earth's water is distributed. Just about all of Earth's water is in the oceans. Ocean water is **salt water.** Land plants and animals, including humans, cannot use salt water. So 97% of Earth's water is not good for people to drink.

To survive, humans need some of the 3% of the water without salt called **fresh water.** After subtracting the frozen water, about 1% of Earth's water remains. This fresh water is in lakes, rivers, groundwater, soil, the atmosphere, and organisms. It is known as free water because it is free to move around the planet. Free water is being refreshed and recycled all the time.

Most of the water we can easily use comes from rivers and lakes. Water in lakes and rivers is known as **surface water.** Water that falls as **precipitation** can either remain as surface water or seep underground where it is stored in soil or porous rock. Underground water is known as groundwater. You can see from the pie chart that there is more water stored underground than at the surface. Groundwater is close at hand, but we can't see it. People drill wells to get groundwater.

Water Use

Americans place high demands on water sources. Think about this. In 1995 people in the United States used about 1,204 billion liters (319 billion gallons) of surface water every day. They also used about 289 billion liters (77 billion gallons) of groundwater every day. That's a total of nearly 1,500 billion liters every day. That works out to about 5,450 liters (1,440 gallons) of water every day for every person in the country!

Of course, you don't use 5,450 liters yourself. But water is needed to grow and prepare food, to make products like paper and cloth, and for hundreds of other uses that benefit you.

People use water in many different ways. Most important, water is essential for life. Without water to drink we wouldn't survive. You can probably think of many nonessential ways you use water at home. You wash your clothes, brush your teeth, and cook your food with water. Swimming pools are filled with water and lawns are watered. Humans also use water for navigation through lakes and rivers, for creating electricity, in manufacturing, and for agriculture. All these activities require a lot of water. No additional water is coming to Earth. And the demand for water continues to grow. How will we survive?

We can't increase the amount of water on Earth. But we can make smart decisions about how much water we remove from natural systems. We can decide how the water is distributed, how it is used, and what happens to it after we use it. As the demand for water increases worldwide due to population increase, everyone will have to **conserve** water.

In California, about 75% of the free water is used for irrigating crops. We can save a lot of water by developing better ways to water crops.

Industry uses a lot of water to make things. Our water supply can be extended by finding ways to reuse and recycle water. Industry must also be careful not to let pollutants get into water supplies.

In the home, water-efficient toilets and washing machines can save a lot of water. Lawns and gardens should be watered at night to reduce water loss to evaporation. Gardens with native plants need little or no water at all. And keep water conservation in mind all the time. Every citizen will have to become more aware of the value of water and treat it as the most precious resource on Earth.

Review Questions

1. **Where is most of Earth's water?**

2. **What are the main sources of fresh water used by humans?**

3. **What can people do to make better use of the water that is available?**

Water vapor is made of individual water molecules. Water vapor enters the air and makes it moist. The moist air moves up in the atmosphere. As moist air rises, it cools. When water vapor cools, it condenses. Water in the atmosphere changes from gas to liquid. Tiny droplets of liquid water form. The condensed water is visible. We recognize condensed water as clouds, fog, and dew.

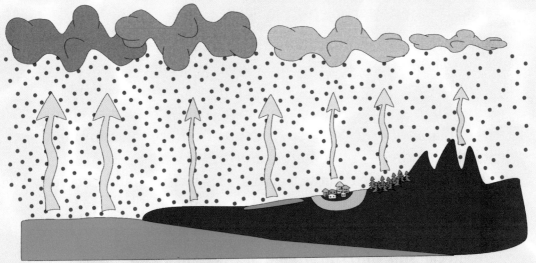

Water vapor condenses in the atmosphere to form clouds.

Water Falls Back to Earth's Surface

Wind blows clouds around. Clouds end up over mountains, forests, cities, deserts, and the ocean. When clouds are loaded with condensed water, the water falls back to Earth's surface as rain. If the temperature is really cold, the water will freeze and fall to Earth's surface as snow, **sleet,** or **hail.**

Water falls back to Earth's surface as rain, snow, sleet, and hail.

Water molecules move through the water cycle at different speeds. And they follow different paths. For example, rain may soak into the soil. A molecule might be taken in by plant roots. It might soon escape into the air through holes in plant leaves. If the air is cool, water might condense immediately as dew and fall back onto the soil. This is a very small water cycle that recycles water back to its starting place quickly.

Rain that lands on the roof of your school may flow to the ground. From there it could enter a stream. After a long journey, it could find its way to the ocean. There the rainwater could reenter the atmosphere as water vapor. By the time it condenses with millions of other molecules to form a drop, the rainwater could be hundreds of kilometers away from where it started. When the molecule returns to Earth's surface, it could fall on the roof of a school in another state. This is an example of a large water cycle that moves water to a new location.

Rain can sink into the ground or freeze in a **glacier.** A molecule far underground or deep in a mass of ice can take a long time to reenter the water cycle. It might take 100 years for a molecule of groundwater to come to the surface in a spring, and even longer for a molecule to break free from a glacier.

The Sun provides the energy to change water into vapor. Water vapor enters the air, where it is carried around the world. When water condenses, gravity pulls it back to Earth's surface. That's the water cycle, and it goes on endlessly.

Review Questions

1. **What is the water cycle?**

2. **When water falls from clouds, what forms can it take?**

3. **Describe a large water cycle that takes a long time to complete.**

4. **Describe a small water cycle that takes a short time to complete.**

ES4b. Students know the influence that the ocean has on the weather and the role that the water cycle plays in weather patterns.

ES4c. Students know the causes and effects of different types of severe weather.

Severe Weather

On August 29, 2005, **Hurricane** Katrina roared across the Gulf of Mexico and onto land. Throughout the country, people watched TV and listened to the radio as Katrina plowed into the states of Louisiana, Mississippi, and Alabama. The wind speed was 255 kilometers per hour (160 miles per hour). The rain poured down. When the storm had passed, hundreds of people were dead, hundreds of thousands were homeless, and the city of New Orleans was flooded. The cost of the damage was in the billions of dollars.

Hurricane Katrina making landfall on the Gulf Coast, August 29, 2005

Weather is fairly predictable most of the time. During the summer months in San Francisco, mornings and afternoons are often foggy. There may be sunshine in the middle of the day. In the winter months, rain is common. In Los Angeles, hot, dry weather is typical in the summer. In Gulf states, summer days are often hot and humid (moist). In the Midwest and East, winters are usually cold, cloudy, and snowy. These are the normal weather conditions that people come to expect where they live.

It's the change from normal to the extreme that catches people's attention. **Tornadoes, thunderstorms,** windstorms, hurricanes, **drought,** and floods are examples of **severe weather.** Severe weather brings out-of-the-ordinary conditions. It may cause dangerous situations that can damage property and threaten lives.

What Is Weather?

We are surrounded by air. It's a little bit like living on the bottom of an ocean of air. Things are always going on in the air surrounding us. The condition of the air around us is what we call weather.

Weather can be described in terms of three important variables. They are heat, moisture, and movement. They are called variables because they change. A day with nice weather might be warm, but not too hot. The sky is clear with just a little bit of moisture in the air. The air is still or moving with a light breeze. That's a perfect day for most people. But not too many days are perfect. Usually it's too hot, too humid, too windy, or too something. But don't worry. Weather always changes.

What Causes Weather to Change?

Energy makes weather happen. Energy makes weather change. The source of energy to create and change weather is the Sun.

When sunshine is intense, the air gets hot. When sunshine is blocked by clouds, or when the Sun goes down, the air cools off.

Moisture in the air takes the form of humidity, clouds, and precipitation. Intense sunshine evaporates more water from Earth's surface. The result is more humidity, more cloud formation, and more rain. When sunshine is less intense, evaporation slows down.

Movement of air is wind. Uneven heating of Earth's surface results in uneven heating of the air touching Earth's surface. Warm air expands and gets less dense. Denser cool air flows under the warm air. This starts a convection current. The air flowing from the cool surface to the warm surface is wind.

Hurricanes and Tropical Storms

Hurricanes are wind systems that rotate around an eye, or center of low atmospheric pressure. Hurricanes form over warm tropical seas. They are classified on a scale from 1 to 5, with 5 being the most powerful storm. Katrina was category 4 as it approached the Gulf Coast of the United States.

Most hurricanes that hit the United States start as tropical storms in the Atlantic Ocean. They form during late summer and early fall when the ocean is warmest. As a tropical storm moves west, it draws energy from the warm water. The storm gets larger, and the wind spins faster and faster.

The spinning wind draws a lot of warm water vapor high in the storm system. When the vapor cools, it condenses. The process of condensation releases even more energy, which makes the system spin even faster. When the hurricane reaches land, the winds are blowing at deadly speeds, up to 250 km/h (155 mph). The rain is very heavy. The wind and rain can cause a lot of destruction.

As soon as a hurricane moves over land, it begins to lose strength. It no longer has warm water to pull energy and water vapor from. Within hours the wind and rain fall to safe levels.

Occasionally hurricanes form in the Pacific Ocean off the coast of Mexico. In 1997 ocean waters along the California coast were warmer than usual. Hurricane Linda formed near Mexico and headed north. Linda was the strongest storm ever recorded in the eastern Pacific, with winds estimated at 290 km/h (180 mph). Fortunately, the storm turned away from California.

Hurricane Linda near Baja California in 1997

Thunderstorms

Thunderstorms form when an air mass at the ground is much warmer and more humid than the air above. Rapid convection begins. As the warm, humid air rises, the water vapor in it condenses. The condensing water vapor releases more heat energy to the surrounding air, causing the air to rise even higher. The rapid movement of air also creates static electric charge on the clouds. When the static electricity discharges, lightning shoots from the clouds to the ground, and you hear the sound of rumbling thunder. Thunderstorms can cause death, start fires, and destroy communications systems. The powerful winds and heavy rain can cause property damage.

Thunderstorms are most common in the afternoon over land. The Sun heats Earth's surface and transfers heat to the air. When cold air flows under the warm air, thunderstorms are possible.

On the afternoon of July 30, 2003, a thunderstorm rolled across Edwards Air Force Base in the Mojave Desert of California. The storm was severe. It broke or uprooted hundreds of trees, damaged roofs of buildings, and caused power outages.

A massive thunderstorm rolling over Edwards AFB

A lightning strike at Edwards AFB

Tornadoes

Tornadoes are powerful forms of wind. They usually happen in late afternoons in spring or summer. When cold air over the land runs into a mass of warm air, the warm air is forced upward violently. At the same time, cooler, denser air flows in from the sides and twists the rising warm air. A spinning funnel forms that "sucks up" everything in its path like a giant vacuum cleaner. The air pressure inside the funnel is very low. The pressure outside the funnel is much higher. The extreme difference in air pressure can create wind speeds of 400 km/h (250 mph) or more. Tornadoes can seriously damage everything in their path.

A tornado rips through a small Texas town.

Tornadoes are most common in the south central part of the country, from Texas to Nebraska. Hundreds of tornadoes occur in this region each year. Warm, moist air from the Gulf of Mexico moves northward. It runs into cooler, drier air flowing down from Canada. This creates perfect conditions for tornadoes. That's why this part of the United States is called Tornado Alley.

Although tornadoes are rare, California does experience them. From 1950 through 2004, 316 tornadoes touched down in California. That's an average of almost six a year.

Hot and Cold

Hot and cold weather are the direct result of solar energy. It gets hot when energy from the Sun is high. It gets cold when solar energy is low. The ocean also affects temperature. The highest and lowest temperatures are never close to the ocean. Water has the ability to absorb and release large amounts of energy without changing temperature much. This keeps places close to the ocean from getting really hot or cold.

Here is a table of temperature extremes for the world, the United States, and California. These temperatures are deadly for most organisms. Only a few tough organisms are able to survive such temperatures.

Range	Location	High Temperature	Low Temperature
World	Al Aziziyah, Libya	58°C (136°F)	
	Vostok, Antarctica		–89°C (–128°F)
United States	Death Valley, California	57°C (134°F)	
	Prospect Creek, Alaska		–62°C (–80°F)
California	Death Valley	57°C (134°F)	
	Boca		–43°C (–45°F)

California Weather Extremes

California does not have many hurricanes and tornadoes. But it does have weather extremes. Most of them involve the ocean.

During the winter, it typically rains and snows in California. When large storms come in from the Pacific Ocean, wind and rain can cause property damage and flooding. In the mountains, the precipitation comes down as snow. Intense snowstorms are called **blizzards.** A single blizzard can drop 4 meters (13 feet) or more of snow. The snow for a whole winter might exceed 10 meters (33 feet).

Meteorologists talk about a weather event called Pineapple Express. It's not a train, but a band of warm, moist air that flows to California from the Hawaiian Islands. When the warm, humid Pineapple Express meets cold air flowing down from Alaska, a violent winter storm can develop. A Pineapple Express rolled into northern California in January 1997. It caused major flooding that filled the Sacramento Valley and caused damage in Yosemite Valley.

The Pineapple Express carries large amounts of moisture to California.

When the Pineapple Express doesn't come to California and the other Pacific storms fail to develop, another kind of extreme weather happens. Drought. Drought is less-than-normal precipitation. In California, drought means less rain along the coast and in the valleys, and much less snow in the mountains.

Less snow means less spring runoff. Less runoff results in reduced flow in rivers and streams. Lakes and ponds shrink and in some cases dry up completely. Soil moisture dries up and groundwater decreases. Reservoirs used to store water for human use shrink.

Droughts stress natural and human communities. Fish and other aquatic organisms may die. Plants that are not adapted for dry environments may die. Reduced water for crops means less food production. People have to conserve water by using less and recycling water when possible.

Serious droughts happened in California from 1929 to 1934, from 1976 to 1977, and from 1987 to 1992. The driest single year ever measured was 1977. In 1991 the Truckee River didn't flow from Lake Tahoe as usual. The level of Lake Tahoe fell below the point where it spilled into the Truckee River.

The Truckee River stopped flowing during the drought of 1991.

The Role of the Ocean in California Weather

The Pacific Ocean affects California's weather in several ways. Most important, the ocean is the source of most of the water used in California. Water evaporates from the ocean, particularly where the Sun has warmed the ocean's surface. Wind carries the water vapor and clouds to California. As the moist air rises and cools over the coastal mountains and the Sierra Nevada, the water condenses and falls back to Earth's surface. During the spring and summer, the water flows back to the ocean, to complete the water cycle.

The ocean creates mild temperatures all year along the California coast. It rarely gets too hot or too cold. The temperature of the ocean doesn't change quickly. So the ocean acts to keep the air temperature near the coast even all year.

The ocean creates breezes near the coast. Because water heats up and cools down slowly, there is often a difference in the temperature of the land and the ocean. Uneven heating starts a convection current in motion, which results in wind. The ocean is responsible for sea breezes.

Review Questions

1. **What causes tornadoes?**
2. **What causes hurricanes?**
3. **How does the water cycle affect weather in California?**
4. **How does the ocean influence the weather in California?**

INVESTIGATION 5

ES4d. Students know how to use weather maps and data to predict local weather and know that weather forecasts depend on many variables.

Weather Maps

Scientists who study weather are called meteorologists. They collect information about the condition of the atmosphere. Meteorologists measure air temperature, moisture content (humidity), and air pressure. They measure wind speed and precipitation. They keep track of the movements of masses of warm and cold air.

But there is more to the meteorologists' job. They want to know more than what the weather is today. They want to predict what the weather will be like tomorrow and the day after tomorrow. Predicting weather is called forecasting.

Meteorologists use information from surface measurements, atmospheric measurements, and satellite images. Information from all three sources is analyzed to make a forecast.

Surface Measurements

Weather data are collected every hour at over 300 stations across the United States. At these locations, meteorologists measure several **weather variables,** including temperature, wind speed and direction, air pressure, cloud cover, and precipitation. These data are fed into weather service computers. The computers generate surface-weather maps.

The surface-weather map has a code at each of the measuring stations. The code is a combination of numbers and symbols. Information about all the weather variables can be read for each station.

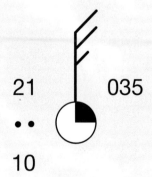

21   035

10

Here's how the information is coded.

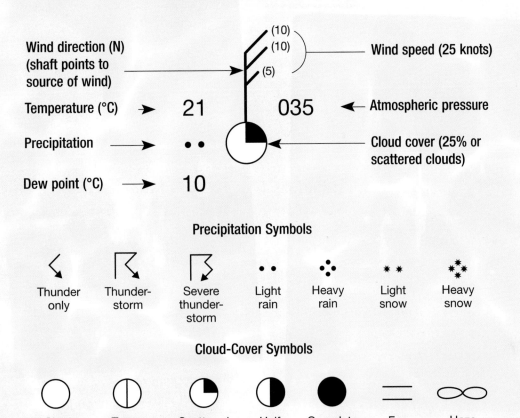

Wind direction (N) (shaft points to source of wind)
(10)
(10)
(5)
Wind speed (25 knots)

Temperature (°C) → 21
035 ← **Atmospheric pressure**

Precipitation → ••
Cloud cover (25% or scattered clouds)

Dew point (°C) → 10

Precipitation Symbols

Thunder only	Thunder-storm	Severe thunder-storm	Light rain	Heavy rain	Light snow	Heavy snow

Cloud-Cover Symbols

Clear	Trace	Scattered clouds	Half cloudy	Complete cloud cover	Fog	Haze

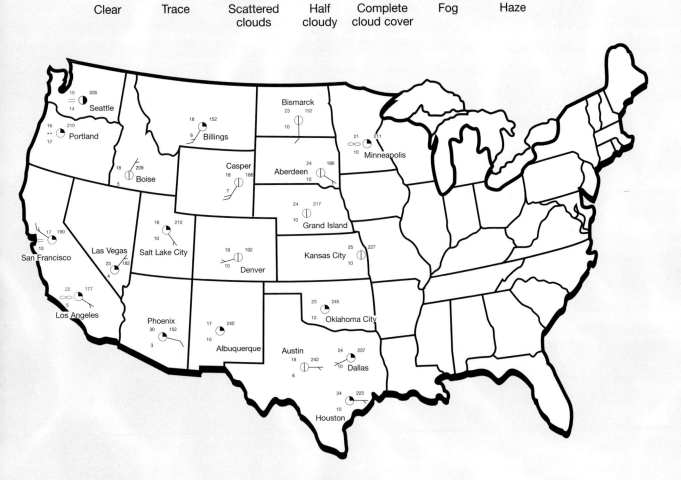

Meteorologists take readings from ground instruments.

Meteorologists release a weather balloon with a radiosonde.

Atmospheric Measurements

Weather balloons carry instruments into the upper atmosphere to make observations twice daily. The balloons are released at exactly the same time all over the world. There are 93 release stations in the United States. In California, the balloons go up at 4:00 a.m. and 4:00 p.m.

The balloons carry **radiosondes,** instruments that measure temperature, pressure, and humidity of the air. The radiosonde sends the information to the station until the balloon pops. Meteorologists also track the balloon's path to figure out wind speed and direction.

Satellite Images

Earth is surrounded by satellites parked in place about 35,000 kilometers (22,000 miles) above Earth's surface. These satellites "watch" the clouds and water vapor move over Earth's surface. They read the temperature of Earth's surface. They identify the storm centers. All this information is sent back to Earth. Meteorologists use powerful computers to change the signals from the satellites into images of Earth's weather.

GOES 8 VIS 18 OCT 00 AT 18:15 UTC   McIDAS

Making Weather Maps

Meteorologists bring together the information from surface measurements, atmospheric measurements, and satellite images. Then they make **weather maps.** A weather map is a way to show weather data as a picture. A basic weather map is a picture of high and low pressure, temperatures, and places where masses of warm and cold air meet. With this information on a map, a meteorologist can make a good weather forecast.

Reading Weather Maps

The Sun heats Earth's surface more near the equator than at the poles. Huge masses of air over the Caribbean Sea become warm. At the same time, huge masses of air in Alaska and northern Canada become cold. The masses of cold air move south, and the masses of warm air move north. When they meet, the area of contact is called a **front.** Weather changes happen at fronts.

A **cold front** happens when a cold air mass overtakes a mass of warm, moist air. When this happens, the cold air pushes under the warm air and pushes it into the upper atmosphere very rapidly. The warm air cools, water condenses, and a thunderstorm occurs. If the temperature difference between the air masses is large, a tornado might develop.

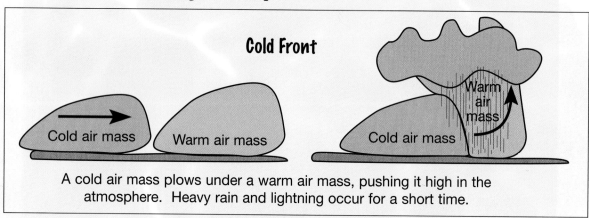

Cold Front

A cold air mass plows under a warm air mass, pushing it high in the atmosphere. Heavy rain and lightning occur for a short time.

A **warm front** happens when a warm air mass overtakes a cold air mass. The warm air slides over the top of the cold air in a long, slanting wedge. The warm air rises and cools slowly, and water vapor condenses into liquid over a long time. Warm fronts produce light rain for a long time.

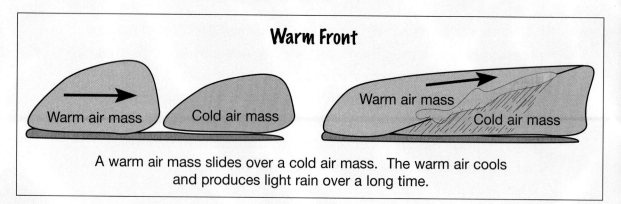

Warm Front

A warm air mass slides over a cold air mass. The warm air cools and produces light rain over a long time.

A line with points on a weather map shows where a cold front is. The points show which direction the cold front is moving. A line with round bumps is used to show where a warm front is. The side of the line with the bumps is the direction the warm front is moving. When the map is prepared in color, cold fronts are blue and warm fronts are red.

Sometimes a warm front and a cold front come together and stop moving. This is called a **stationary front.** It is shown by a line with points on one side and bumps on the other. The weather under a stationary front is similar to the weather produced by a cold front.

High-pressure areas are shown on a weather map with a large letter *H.* Low-pressure areas are shown by a large letter *L.*

H   L

The weather around a high-pressure center is usually cool and dry. That's because high pressure is associated with denser air. Denser air tends to be cool and dry.

Low-pressure areas are usually warmer and moist. That's because low pressure is associated with less-dense air.

When a low-pressure area is near a high-pressure area, air will move from the high-pressure area to the low-pressure area. The movement of air is wind. The weather around a low-pressure area is windy and possibly rainy. As the warm air rises, cools, and condenses into clouds, it could start to rain.

Look at the three weather maps for Monday, September 19, 2005. Look at the large cold front going from Texas to New York. The upper part of the front moves across several states in the East. The southern end of the front, however, is stationary.

In map 1, a cold front meets a warm front in Canada. Warm, moist air rises and condenses. The forecast is for rain.

In map 2, a low-pressure area developed over the Dakotas Monday afternoon. Air from the high-pressure area over the Rocky Mountains in Colorado might flow across Wyoming and Nebraska to the low-pressure area. The forecast is for wind.

Look at map 3. What is the weather in California? There is a low-pressure area in southern California. Cool, moist air from the ocean is flowing toward the low-pressure area. If the moist air warms and rises as it approaches the warm low-pressure area, it could cool and condense. The forecast is for clouds and possible showers.

Look in the lower right-hand corner of the maps. There is a symbol that looks like this.

That is the symbol for a tropical storm or hurricane. This is Hurricane Rita. It is traveling past the southern tip of Florida not even a month after Hurricane Katrina hit the Gulf Coast. The forecast is for extreme wind and rain.

**Monday
morning
8:00 a.m.**

Map 1

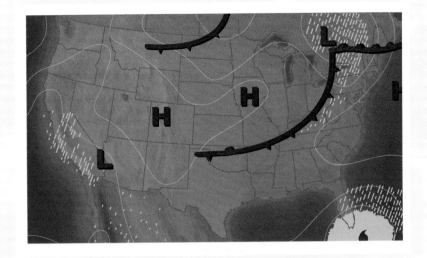

**Monday
afternoon
2:00 p.m.**

Map 2

**Monday
evening
8:00 p.m.**

Map 3

At National Weather Service forecast offices all around the United States, meteorologists use their skill and experience to produce weather forecasts. They consider all the weather variables such as air pressure, temperature, moisture, and wind. And they use their knowledge of general weather patterns.

Meteorologists know that winds in the upper atmosphere blow from west to east over most of the United States. So they know that most big weather systems also move from west to east.

They also know that air flows from high-pressure areas to low-pressure areas. This creates wind. So they look for high- and low-pressure areas on the weather map to figure out which way and how hard the wind will blow.

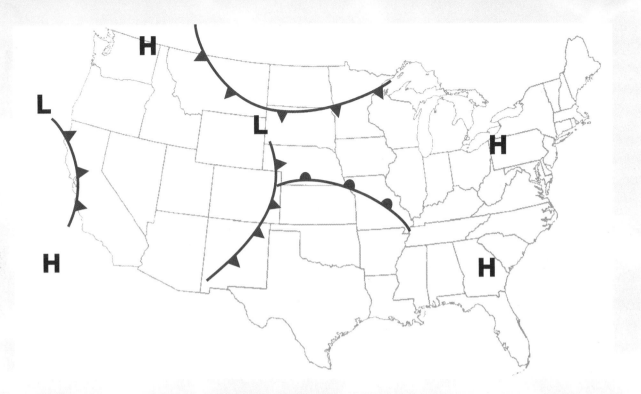

Review Questions

1. **What weather variables do meteorologists measure when they are preparing to make a weather forecast?**

2. **Describe three kinds of fronts and the weather they produce.**

3. **What causes wind?**

4. **Look at the sample weather map above. Where do you think it is raining? Where will it be raining tomorrow?**

5. **Look at the high- and low-pressure centers on the map above. Where do you think the wind is blowing? What direction?**

6. **Where is it likely to be cold and dry?**

California Water Map

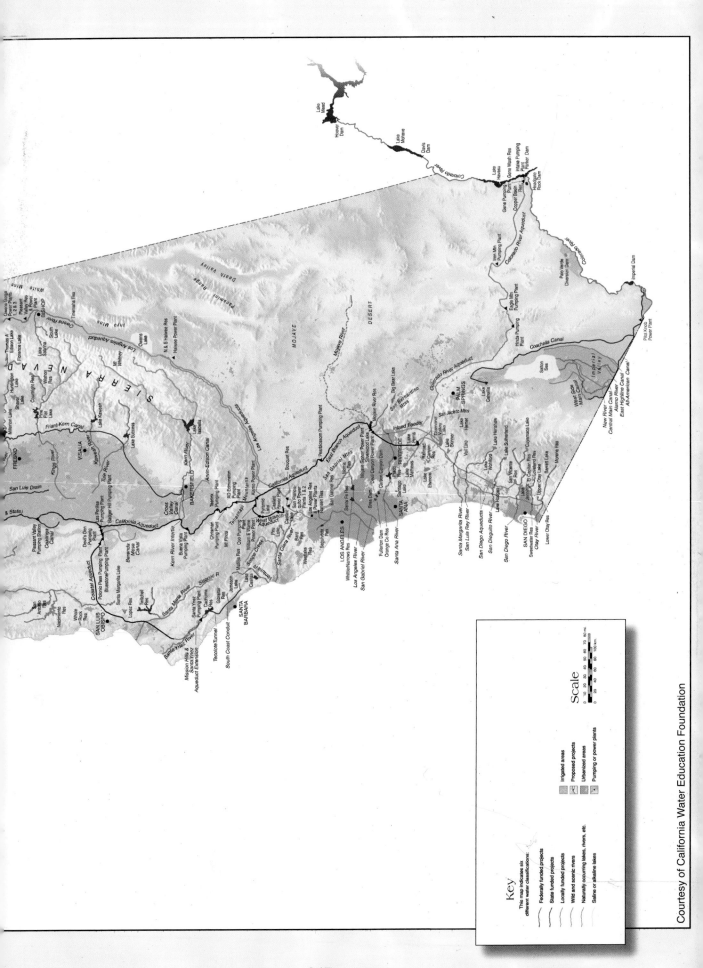

247

Courtesy of California Water Education Foundation

Summary: Weather

Earth has weather. Three things cause the weather. First, Earth is just 150 million kilometers (93 million miles) away from a star, the Sun. Sunshine is the energy source that makes weather happen.

Second, Earth has an atmosphere made of air. This is where weather happens. Weather is what's happening in the atmosphere at any given time and place.

Third, Earth has water. Seventy-one percent of Earth's surface is covered by water. Most of Earth's weather has something to do with water.

Water Cycle

One thing weather does is move water around the planet. Most of Earth's water is **salt water.** Only 3% is **fresh water.** And only a small amount of the fresh water is available to plants and animals living on the land surfaces of Earth. People depend on that little bit of Earth's water for survival.

Will we run out of water? No, because it is recycled all the time by the **water cycle.** Water on Earth's surface evaporates and enters the atmosphere as water vapor, a gas. The most important source of evaporating water is the oceans. When water vapor rises in the atmosphere and cools, it condenses into liquid water. Clouds made of countless droplets of water drift around the planet. When droplets form drops or ice crystals, they fall back to Earth's surface as **rain, snow, sleet,** or **hail.**

Severe Weather

Weather is defined by several **weather variables.** Weather variables describe the conditions of the atmosphere in a location on Earth. They include temperature, humidity, pressure, wind, and precipitation. Most of the time these variables fall within safe and comfortable limits. The weather might be rainy and windy, but not dangerous.

Sometimes one or more weather variables become extreme. This results in **severe weather.** Examples of severe weather include **tornadoes, hurricanes, thunderstorms, drought,** heat, and cold. Severe weather is dangerous to living organisms and can destroy property.

Hurricanes are powerful storms that form over warm water in late summer. The winds circling a hurricane's eye can reach speeds of 250 kilometers per hour (155 miles per hour). The energy that drives the storm is drawn from ocean water heated by the Sun. When a hurricane reaches land, the destruction caused by the wind and the flooding can be terrible.

A hurricane

A tornado

Thunderstorms and tornadoes form when a warm air mass and a cold air mass meet. The warm air is pushed upward rapidly. Lightning and heavy rain follow. When conditions are right, a spinning tornado can form. Winds in a tornado can reach speeds of more than 400 kilometers per hour (250 miles per hour). This makes tornadoes violent and dangerous storms on Earth.

Meteorologists study weather. One thing they try to do is to predict what the weather will be in the future. This is called forecasting. To make accurate forecasts, meteorologists have to collect a lot of weather data. Data are collected in three ways. Meteorologists measure weather variables at Earth's surface in hundreds of locations using weather instruments. They measure weather variables in the atmosphere in hundreds of locations, using weather balloons and **radiosondes.** And they study images sent to Earth by weather satellites. All of these data are sent to supercomputers.

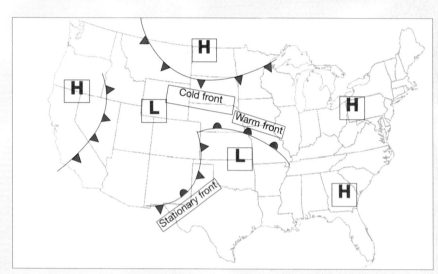

Meteorologists then make **weather maps** from the computer output. A weather map is a picture of the conditions of the atmosphere. It shows the high- and low-pressure areas. It shows where it is raining or snowing.

It shows **warm fronts, cold fronts,** and **stationary fronts.** Experienced meteorologists can use weather maps to forecast the next day's weather.

Summary Questions

Now is a good time to review what you have recorded in your science notebook. Think about the weather investigations you conducted.

1. **Where is the water on Earth?**

2. **Describe how California's water supply is refreshed by the water cycle.**

3. **What are some of the ways the ocean affects weather?**

California Science Standards

ES3a. Students know most of Earth's water is present as salt water in the oceans, which cover most of Earth's surface.

ES3c. Students know water vapor in the air moves from one place to another and can form fog or clouds, which are tiny droplets of water or ice, and can fall to Earth as rain, hail, sleet, or snow.

ES3d. Students know that the amount of fresh water located in rivers, lakes, under-ground sources, and glaciers is limited and that its availability can be extended by recycling and decreasing the use of water.

ES4b. Students know the influence that the ocean has on the weather and the role that the water cycle plays in weather patterns.

ES4c. Students know the causes and effects of different types of severe weather.

ES4d. Students know how to use weather maps and data to predict local weather and know that weather forecasts depend on many variables.

Vocabulary

salt water

fresh water

water cycle

rain

snow

sleet

hail

weather variables

severe weather

tornado

hurricane

thunderstorm

drought

radiosonde

weather map

warm front

cold front

stationary front

Learning More about the Water Planet

The Planets

Visit a Planetarium

If there is a planetarium in your community, plan a visit. Check for presentations on the solar system, space exploration, or specific planets.

Plan a Visit with a Sidewalk Astronomer

You will find sidewalk astronomers in many communities who are willing to share their telescopes and knowledge. Visit the CA FOSSweb site for sidewalk astronomy resources.

Create a Travel Brochure

Choose a planet you would visit if you could. Design a travel brochure with descriptions of features, images, and tour information. Come up with a tour cost, too.

Find Out about Eratosthenes

Eratosthenes was a librarian who lived in Greece during the 3rd century B.C.E. He was the first person to calculate the circumference of Earth. Find out how Eratosthenes measured Earth and what effect his calculations might have had on Christopher Columbus's voyage to the Americas. *The Librarian Who Measured the Earth* by Kathryn Lasky is a good book to start with.

Create a Space-Exploration Timeline

Research the history of space exploration by the United States and other countries. Create a timeline that includes major events in space exploration.

Variables

Investigate Linked Pendulums

A double pendulum provides lots of interesting variables to investigate. Hang two equal pendulums next to each other and connect them with a straw that has been split at each end. Investigate changing the release positions and release times of the two pendulums. Add more mass to one pendulum, and change the angle of the straw.

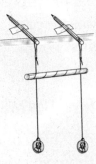

Investigate Stringless Pendulums

Replace the pendulum string with some kind of rigid material. Compare pendulums made with rulers, sticks, straws, paper-clip chains, or wire.

Make two pendulums the same length, one constructed in the usual way and one made with a ruler. Compare these pendulums. Does something seem peculiar? What happens to the period of the cycle of the two pendulums as the mass of the bob increases? Consult a reference to figure out what is going on.

Weather and Water

Research Recycling Water

The National Aeronautics and Space Administration (NASA) is working on ways to recycle water for astronauts in space. Research how NASA plans to do this.

- How many ways do astronauts use water?

- Why is it important for them to be able to recycle water?

Research Water Storage and Delivery Systems

Many areas of the United States store water in reservoirs. Find out where your water is stored and how it gets to your home and school. What effect does evaporation have on water storage?

Find the Condensation Temperature

Water vapor will not condense on a cup of warm water. Water vapor will condense on a cup of ice water. Somewhere between warm water and ice water is the temperature at which vapor will first condense. Find that temperature. The temperature is called dew point.

Investigate Solar Heating of Different Materials

Think of earth materials that have properties different from those you studied in class. Find out how the different properties affect temperature change. You might start with light and dark sand or water of different colors.

Research Temperatures around the World

Use the newspaper to keep track of temperatures for five California cities for 2 weeks. Compare temperature data from coastal cities and inland cities. Which cities have the biggest temperature variations? Why? Pick a city and graph its temperature day by day all year.

Look for Severe Weather Now

Severe weather is occurring somewhere right now. Go to a news source or weather website to find out about severe windstorms (tornadoes, cyclones, monsoons, typhoons), heavy thunderstorms, and temperature extremes. Use a world map to display the current weather extremes. (Often California is the hottest place on Earth during the summer.)

Earth Sciences Glossary

Air   The mixture of gases surrounding Earth.

Asteroid   Small, solid objects that orbit the Sun. Most of the asteroids in the solar system are located between Mars and Jupiter.

Astronomy   The study of the universe and its celestial bodies.

Atmosphere   The layer of gases that surrounds a planet or star.

Atmospheric pressure   The force exerted on a surface by the mass of the air above it.

Atom   The smallest particle of an element that has the properties of the element and can exist either alone or in combination with a similar atom as a molecule.

Blizzard   A severe storm with low temperatures, strong winds, and large quantities of snow.

Bob   A mass at the end of a pendulum.

Chemical property   A characteristic of an element that relates to how it interacts with other elements.

Cloud   Tiny droplets of water, usually high in the air.

Cold front   The contact zone where a cold air mass overtakes a mass of warm, moist air.

Comet   A mass of ice and dust orbiting the Sun.

Condensation   The process by which water vapor changes into liquid water, usually on a surface.

Conserve   To use carefully and protect.

Controlled experiment   A scientific test where only one variable can change.

Controlled variable   Any variable in an experiment that is not allowed to change.

Convection current A circular movement of fluid (such as air) that is the result of uneven heating of the fluid.

Crater A hole formed by an object impacting a surface.

Cycle A set of events or actions that repeats.

Data Information collected and recorded as a result of observation.

Dependent variable What you find out as a result of doing an experiment.

Dew Water that condenses on surfaces when the temperature drops at night.

Diameter The straight-line distance from one side to the other side of an object through the center.

Drought Less-than-normal amount of rain or snow over a period of time.

Earth The third planet from the Sun, known as the water planet.

Elevation The distance above sea level.

Energy transfer The movement of energy from one place to another, or the change of energy from one form to another.

Evaporate To change from liquid to gas.

Evaporation The process by which a liquid becomes a gas.

Extraterrestrial Beyond Earth.

Fog Water droplets that condense from the air close to the ground.

Forecasting Predicting future events or conditions, such as weather.

Freezing point The temperature at which a liquid turns into a solid (also the same temperature as the melting point).

Fresh water Water without salt that is found in lakes, rivers, groundwater, soil, and the atmosphere.

Front The leading edge of a moving air mass.

Frost Frozen condensation.

Gas   A state of a substance with no definite shape or volume.

Gas giant   Any of the four planets that are made of gas. These are Jupiter, Saturn, Uranus, and Neptune.

Glacier   A huge mass of ice that moves slowly over land.

Gravitational attraction   The mutual force of attraction between all bodies that have mass.

Gravity   The force of attraction between two objects.

Hail   Precipitation in the form of small balls or pellets of ice.

Helium   A gas that makes up 26% of the Sun.

Humidity   Water vapor in the air.

Hurricane   A severe tropical storm or moving wind system that rotates around an eye.

Hydrogen   A gas that makes up 72% of the Sun.

Independent variable   The variable in an experiment that you control the value of in advance.

Intensity   How concentrated energy is.

Jupiter   The fifth planet from the Sun.

Kuiper Belt   A huge region beyond the gas giants made up of different-size icy chunks of matter.

Liquid   A state of a substance with no definite shape but definite volume.

Mars   The fourth planet from the Sun.

Mass   The amount of material in something.

Mercury   The planet closest to the Sun.

Meteorologist   A scientist who studies the weather.

Milky Way   The galaxy in which the solar system resides.

Moon   Earth's natural satellite.

Neptune   The eighth planet from the Sun.

Orbit   To travel in a curved path around something else.

Pendulum   A mass on one end of an arm that is free to swing back and forth in response to gravity.

Period   The length of time it takes for a pendulum to complete a cycle.

Planet   A large body orbiting a star. A celestial body.

Pluto   A dwarf planet in the Kuiper Belt.

Precipitation   Rain, snow, sleet, or hail that falls to the ground.

Predict   To estimate a future event based on data or experience.

Predictable   Possible to estimate a future event based on data or experience.

Radiosonde   An instrument sent into Earth's atmosphere to measure temperature, pressure, and humidity.

Rain   Liquid water that is condensed from water vapor in the atmosphere and falls to Earth in drops.

Recycle   To use again.

Reflected   Energy that bounces off an object and continues in a new direction.

Salt water   Ocean water.

Satellite   An object, natural or artificial, that orbits a larger object. Moons are satellites.

Saturated   When the air cannot hold any more water vapor.

Saturn   The sixth planet from the Sun.

Severe weather   Out-of-the-ordinary and extreme weather conditions.

Sleet   Precipitation in the form of ice pellets created when rain freezes as it falls to Earth from the atmosphere.

Snow   Precipitation in the form of ice crystals grouped together as snowflakes.

Solar energy   Heat and light from the Sun.

Solar system   The planet Earth, the Moon, the Sun, and seven other planets and their satellites, and smaller objects, such as asteroids and comets.

Solar wind The regular flow of particles from the Sun.

Star A huge gas sphere that radiates light. The Sun is a star.

Stationary front When a warm air mass and a cold air mass come together and stop moving.

Sun The star at the center of the solar system around which everything else orbits. Also called Sol.

Surface area The amount of space covering the topmost layer of water or land.

Surface water Fresh water on Earth's surface, such as that in lakes and rivers.

Terrestrial planet One of the four small and rocky planets closest to the Sun. These are Mercury, Venus, Earth, and Mars.

Thermonuclear reactions Reactions that change atomic structure and create heat and light energy, such as the reactions that occur on the Sun.

Thunderstorm Severe weather that results from cold air flowing under a warm, humid air mass over the land.

Tornado A rapidly rotating column of air that extends from a thunderstorm to the ground. Wind speeds can reach 417 kilometers per hour (260 mph) or more in a tornado.

Two-coordinate graph A plot of the relationship between an independent variable on the x-axis and a dependent variable on the y-axis.

Uneven heating The result of different amounts of energy being transferred to adjacent surfaces.

Uranus The seventh planet from the Sun.

Variable Anything you can change in an experiment that might affect the outcome.

Venus The second planet from the Sun.

Warm front The contact zone where a warm air mass overtakes a cold air mass.

Water cycle   The global water-recycling system. Water evaporates from Earth's surface, goes into the atmosphere, and condenses. It returns to Earth's surface as precipitation in a new location.

Water molecule   Two hydrogen atoms and one oxygen atom bonded together.

Water vapor   Water in its gas form.

Weather   The condition of the atmosphere around us. Heat, moisture, and movement are the three important variables that describe weather.

Weather forecast   A prediction of future weather conditions.

Weather map   A map that shows weather data as a picture.

Weather variable   Data that meteorologists measure. These include temperature, wind speed and direction, air pressure, cloud cover, and precipitation.

Wind   Air in motion.

X-axis   The horizontal number line of a two-coordinate graph.

Y-axis   The vertical number line of a two-coordinate graph.

References

Table of Contents

References

Science Safety Rules

1. Listen carefully to your teacher's instructions. Follow all directions. Ask questions if you don't know what to do.

2. Tell your teacher if you have any allergies.

3. Never put any materials in your mouth. Do not taste anything unless your teacher tells you to do so.

4. Never smell any unknown material. If your teacher tells you to smell something, wave your hand over the material to bring the smell toward your nose.

5. Do not touch your face, mouth, ears, eyes, or nose while working with chemicals, plants, or animals.

6. Always protect your eyes. Wear safety goggles when necessary. Tell your teacher if you wear contact lenses.

7. Always wash your hands with soap and warm water after handling chemicals, plants, or animals.

8. Never mix any chemicals unless your teacher tells you to do so.

9. Report all spills, accidents, and injuries to your teacher.

10. Treat animals with respect, caution, and consideration.

11. Clean up your work space after each investigation.

12. Act responsibly during all science activities.

CA FOSSweb

Go to www.FOSSweb.com/CA to find activities for each FOSS module. You will also find interesting books to read, vocabulary lists, and links to related websites. This site was designed for you to use with friends and family at home. For your parents, there is information about each FOSS module and copies of the Home/School Connections.

California Science Content Standards for Grade 5

Physical Sciences

1. Elements and their combinations account for all the varied types of matter in the world. As a basis for understanding this concept:

   a. *Students know* that during chemical reactions the atoms in the reactants rearrange to form products with different properties.

   b. *Students know* all matter is made of atoms, which may combine to form molecules.

   c. *Students know* metals have properties in common, such as high electrical and thermal conductivity. Some metals, such as aluminum (Al), iron (Fe), nickel (Ni), copper (Cu), silver (Ag), and gold (Au), are pure elements; others, such as steel and brass, are composed of a combination of elemental metals.

   d. *Students know* that each element is made of one kind of atom and that the elements are organized in the periodic table by their chemical properties.

   e. *Students know* scientists have developed instruments that can create discrete images of atoms and molecules that show that the atoms and molecules often occur in well-ordered arrays.

   f. *Students know* differences in chemical and physical properties of substances are used to separate mixtures and identify compounds.

   g. *Students know* properties of solid, liquid, and gaseous substances, such as sugar ($C_6H_{12}O_6$), water (H_2O), helium (He), oxygen (O_2), nitrogen (N_2), and carbon dioxide (CO_2).

   h. *Students know* living organisms and most materials are composed of just a few elements.

   i. *Students know* the common properties of salts, such as sodium chloride (NaCl).

265

Life Sciences

2. Plants and animals have structures for respiration, digestion, waste disposal, and transport of materials. As a basis for understanding this concept:

   a. *Students know* many multicellular organisms have specialized structures to support the transport of materials.

   b. *Students know* how blood circulates through the heart chambers, lungs, and body and how carbon dioxide (CO_2) and oxygen (O_2) are exchanged in the lungs and tissues.

   c. *Students know* the sequential steps of digestion and the roles of teeth and the mouth, esophagus, stomach, small intestine, large intestine, and colon in the function of the digestive system.

   d. *Students know* the role of the kidney in removing cellular waste from blood and converting it into urine, which is stored in the bladder.

   e. *Students know* how sugar, water, and minerals are transported in a vascular plant.

   f. *Students know* plants use carbon dioxide (CO_2) and energy from sunlight to build molecules of sugar and release oxygen.

   g. *Students know* plant and animal cells break down sugar to obtain energy, a process resulting in carbon dioxide (CO_2) and water (respiration).

Earth Sciences

3. Water on Earth moves between the oceans and land through the processes of evaporation and condensation. As a basis for understanding this concept:

   a. *Students know* most of Earth's water is present as salt water in the oceans, which cover most of Earth's surface.

   b. *Students know* when liquid water evaporates, it turns into water vapor in the air and can reappear as a liquid when cooled or as a solid if cooled below the freezing point of water.

c. *Students know* water vapor in the air moves from one place to another and can form fog or clouds, which are tiny droplets of water or ice, and can fall to Earth as rain, hail, sleet, or snow.

d. *Students know* that the amount of fresh water located in rivers, lakes, underground sources, and glaciers is limited and that its availability can be extended by recycling and decreasing the use of water.

e. *Students know* the origin of the water used by their local communities.

4. Energy from the Sun heats Earth unevenly, causing air movements that result in changing weather patterns. As a basis for understanding this concept:

a. *Students know* uneven heating of Earth causes air movements (convection currents).

b. *Students know* the influence that the ocean has on the weather and the role that the water cycle plays in weather patterns.

c. *Students know* the causes and effects of different types of severe weather.

d. *Students know* how to use weather maps and data to predict local weather and know that weather forecasts depend on many variables.

e. *Students know* that the Earth's atmosphere exerts a pressure that decreases with distance above Earth's surface and that at any point it exerts this pressure equally in all directions.

5. The solar system consists of planets and other bodies that orbit the Sun in predictable paths. As a basis for understanding this concept:

a. *Students know* the Sun, an average star, is the central and largest body in the solar system and is composed primarily of hydrogen and helium.

b. *Students know* the solar system includes the planet Earth, the Moon, the Sun, eight other planets and their satellites, and smaller objects, such as asteroids and comets.

c. *Students know* the path of a planet around the Sun is due to the gravitational attraction between the Sun and the planet.

Investigation and Experimentation

6. Scientific progress is made by asking meaningful questions and conducting careful investigations. As a basis for understanding this concept and addressing the content in the other three strands, students should develop their own questions and perform investigations. Students will:

   a. Classify objects (e.g., rocks, plants, leaves) in accordance with appropriate criteria.

   b. Develop a testable question.

   c. Plan and conduct a simple investigation based on a student-developed question and write instructions others can follow to carry out the procedure.

   d. Identify the dependent and controlled variables in an investigation.

   e. Identify a single independent variable in a scientific investigation and explain how this variable can be used to collect information to answer a question about the results of the experiment.

   f. Select appropriate tools (e.g., thermometers, meter sticks, balances, and graduated cylinders) and make quantitative observations.

   g. Record data by using appropriate graphic representations (including charts, graphs, and labeled diagrams) and make inferences based on those data.

   h. Draw conclusions from scientific evidence and indicate whether further information is needed to support a specific conclusion.

   i. Write a report of an investigation that includes conducting tests, collecting data or examining evidence, and drawing conclusions.

Photo Credits

Cover: © CORBIS **Page 1:** Science VU/IBMRL/Visuals Unlimited; **Page 3:** Lawrence Hall of Science (top); © David Duran/Fundamental Photographs (bottom, both); **Page 4:** Lawrence Hall of Science (all); **Page 5:** Corel Corporation (top); © Charles D. Winters/TimeFrame Photography, Inc./Photo Researchers, Inc. (bottom right); Lawrence Hall of Science (bottom left); **Pages 6–17:** Lawrence Hall of Science (all); **Page 18:** © Paul Silverman/Fundamental Photographs; **Pages 19, 21:** Lawrence Hall of Science (all); **Page 22:** CORBIS (top); Lawrence Hall of Science (bottom); **Pages 23, 25, 28:** Lawrence Hall of Science; **Page 34:** Lawrence Hall of Science (left); © Doug Sokell/Visuals Unlimited; **Page 36:** © Brand X Pictures/Fotosearch; **Page 43:** Public image; **Pages 45–46, 48–49:** Lawrence Hall of Science; **Page 50:** National Portrait Gallery, London; **Page 51:** Brown Brothers; **Page 52:** © David Wrobel/Visuals Unlimited (left); © Breck P. Kent (center inset); © C.P. George/Visuals Unlimited (right); **Page 53:** © Charles D. Winters/Photo Researchers, Inc. (top); © Science VU/Alcan/Visuals Unlimited (bottom); **Page 54:** © Ken Lucas/Visuals Unlimited (top); © Jeff Greenberg/Visuals Unlimited (bottom); **Page 55:** © Jeff J. Daly/Visuals Unlimited (top left, bottom right); © Breck P. Kent (top right, bottom left); **Page 56:** Mining Foundation Southwest/Fotosmith; **Page 57:** © Breck P. Kent (top left inset; bottom right, second from bottom inset); © Astrid & Hanns-Frieder/Science Photo Library (top right inset); © Bruce Berg/Visuals Unlimited (center right); © Russ Lapa/Photo Researchers, Inc. (bottom right inset); © John D. Cunningham/Visuals Unlimited (bottom left); **Page 58:** Lawrence Hall of Science; **Page 59:** Hubble Heritage Team/NASA; **Page 60:** Lawrence Hall of Science; **Page 62:** NASA; **Page 63:** Lawrence Hall of Science; **Page 64:** © Dr. Joseph A. Stroscio/National Institute of Standards and Technology (top right); © BMRL/Visuals Unlimited (bottom right); **Page 65:** Lawrence Hall of Science (both); **Page 66:** Lawrence Hall of Science (top left); Lawrence Berkeley Laboratory (right); **Pages 67–68:** Lawrence Hall of Science (all); **Page 73:** © Jeff G. Daly (top left); Lawrence Hall of Science (center right and bottom left); **Page 74:** Science VU/IBMRL/Visuals Unlimited; **Page 83:** © Phillip Colla/oceanlight.com; **Page 85:** © M. I. Walker/Photo Researchers, Inc. (top left); James Richardson/Visuals Unlimited (top right); Dr. Gladden Willis/Visuals Unlimited (bottom); **Page 86:** © M. I. Walker/Photo Researchers, Inc.; **Page 87:** © Russell Kightly/Photo Researchers, Inc. (top); © Andrew Syred/Photo Researchers, Inc. (bottom); **Page 88:** Rose Craig/Lawrence Hall of Science (both); **Page 89:** Rose Craig/Lawrence Hall of Science (top); Dr. Gladden Willis/Visuals Unlimited (bottom); **Page 91:** Lawrence Hall of Science; **Pages 92–93:** Rose Craig/Lawrence Hall of Science; **Page 95:** © Phillip Colla/oceanlight.com; **Pages 96–97, 99:** Rose Craig/Lawrence Hall of Science (all); **Page 100:** © John Gerlach/Earth Scenes; **Page 101:** © Biodisc/Visuals Unlimited (top); Lawrence Hall of Science (bottom left); Bruce Iverson (bottom right); **Pages 102–107:** Rose Craig/Lawrence Hall of Science; **Page 108:** Lawrence Hall of Science (top left); © Biodisc/Visuals Unlimited (top right); Rose Craig/Lawrence Hall of Science (bottom); **Page 111, 115–116:** Rose Craig/Lawrence Hall of Science (all); **Page 122:** © David Young-Wolff/Photo Edit, Inc. (left); Mike Dehoog/Sports Chrome (right); **Page 123:** OLDWAYS Preservation Trust (top); Robert Fried (center); © Michelle D. Bridwell/Photo Edit, Inc. (bottom right); **Page 124:** OLDWAYS Preservation Trust (top); © Fujifotos/The Image Works (center left); © David R. Frazier/Photo Researchers, Inc. (bottom right); **Page 125:** OLDWAYS Preservation Trust (top); © Todd Gipstein/CORBIS (center); Lawrence Migdale (bottom); **Page 126:** Lawrence Migdale; **Page 131:** Rose Craig/Lawrence Hall of Science; **Page 143:** NASA; **Page 145:** Rose Craig/Lawrence Hall of Science; **Page 146:** NASA/JPL; **Page 148:** Lawrence Hall of Science (top); NASA/JPL/Northwestern University (bottom); **Pages 149–151:** NASA/JPL (all); **Page 152:** NASA/JPL/USGS (top); NASA/JPL; **Page 153:** Dennis diCicco/CORBIS/JPL (background, top right, center left, middle and right); NASA/JPL/University of Arizona (bottom left); **Page 154:** NASA/JPL (both); **Page 155:** NASA/Hubble Space Telescope (left); NASA/JPL (right); **Page 156:** NASA/JPL (top); NASA/JPL-Caltech (bottom); **Page 157:** Dennis diCicco/CORBIS (top); NASA/Hubble Space Telescope (center); NASA (bottom); **Page 159:** NASA/JPL (left); Courtesy, Ellen Lopez (right); **Pages 160–161:** Rose Craig/Lawrence Hall of Science; **Pages 162–163:**

About the Cover: A field of California poppies

Index

Chemical properties, 199. *See also*
    Physical properties
  color and, 47
  defined, 78, 255
  and elements, 43
  elements organized by, 75
  of metals, 52
  in periodic table, 72
  and predicting unknown elements, 44
  separating mixtures and identifying
    compounds, 14, 26
  similarities among elements, 43–44
Chemical reaction
  atoms and, 39
  from baking soda and hydrochloric
    acid, 32
  defined, 29, 40, 78
Chemists, 68–71
Chicago, Illinois, 162
Chlorine (Cl), 33, 50, 60
  atom, 32
Chlorophyll, 115, 116, 131, 138
Chromatography, 70
Chromium (Cr), 54, 57
Circular current, 205. *See also* Convection
  current
Circular orbits, 161, 165
Circulate, 87, 138
Circulatory system
  defined, 138
  gas exchange in lungs and cells, 89–90
  how cells get resources, 86
  left side of heart, 88
  main parts of, 90, 96
  resource delivery, 87
  right side of heart, 88
Citric acid, 28, 31, 76
Citric acid solution, 28
Classification, 105–106, 138
Classify, 108, 134, 138
Clouds
  changing weather, 228
  -cover symbols, 237

defined, 225, 255
forecast for, 242–243
of Jupiter, 153
and liquid water, 189–191, 194
of Neptune, 155
and rain, 242
role of ocean in California, 234
satellite images of, 239
and solar energy, 199
in space, 159
of Uranus, 155
water cycle, 248, 251
weather in Midwest and East, 227
as weather variable, 236–237
Cobalt (Co), 57
Cold
  as basic property, 42
  weather in Midwest and East, 227
Cold air, 186
Cold front, 240–243, 250, 255
Cold saturated solution, 25
Collect, 112
Colon, 92, 97, 138
Color and the Sun, 199
Colorado, 242
Comet, 157, 164, 165, 167, 255
Comet Shoemaker-Levy, 9, 157
Compounds, 36, 39, 78
Computers, 239, 250
Conclusion, 111, 114
Condensation, 189–195. *See also*
  Evaporation; Water vapor
  defined, 189, 194, 255
  finding temperature of, 254
  in hurricanes and tropical storms, 229
  water and, 225, 226
  water vapor and, 194–195
Conduct, 76–77, 111–112, 136
Conservation, 222, 234
Conserve, 255

temperature and, 232
temperature of, 214
temperature of water, 200
water cycle, 248, 251
Octane
chemical formula for, 37–38
defined, 80
equation for burning, 38
Oils, 60, 118, 121–122, 125
Opportunity, 151
Orbits, 145
of asteroids around Sun, 164
circular, 165
of comets around Sun, 157, 164
defined, 257
of planets around Sun, 164, 167
predictable, 147
of satellites around Sun, 164
of space shuttle around Earth, 163
Orderly arrays, 64
Ore
bauxite, 53
defined, 52, 80
and precious metals, 55
uranium, 51
Oxidation, 54, 57
Oxidize, 52, 54–55, 80
Oxygen (O)
as abundant element, 62–63
in air molecule, 194
atom, 31, 33, 35
in baking soda, 32
and carbohydrates, 117
and cells, 87, 96
cells need, 89
and cellular respiration, 119
chemical formula for, 35
defined, 140
on Earth, 33
in Earth's atmosphere, 150
gas, 31
in human body, 60–61, 73
and hydrogen, 37
and iron, 34
making food, 112–114

molecules (O_2), 30–31, 33, 36, 116, 183–185
and photosynthesis, 115–117, 131–132
properties, 26
pure, 33
reaction with carbon, 29–30
and respiratory system, 90
testing effect of, 28–29
as unchangeable element, 43
in water molecule, 184–185
when metal oxidizes, 52
Ozone layer, 70

P

Pacific Ocean, 220, 229, 232–235
Palmate, 105, 108, 140
Pancreas, 127, 140
Parallel, 105, 108, 140
Particles. *See also* Atoms; Molecules
air, 20
atomic, 65
citric acid, 31
defined, 25, 80
dissolved salt, 10
powder, 8
salt, 16–18, 25
size of, 8, 13
sodium chloride, 16
in Solar System, 59
water, 25
Patterns, weather, 244
Peace Corps, 162
Pendulum
defined, 257
Galileo's experiment, 169–171, 178–179
investigation of linked and stringless, 253
Period, 169–171, 258
Periodic table of the elements, 42–49
defined, 72, 80
information in, 73
organization of elements in, 75

Volume
  defined, 81
  gases, 5
  solids and liquids, 4, 16, 18

W

Warm air, 186
Warm front, 240–243, 250, 259
Waste, cellular, 93–94, 97. *See also*
  Excretory system
Waste chemicals, 93, 97
Waste disposal, 86, 95, 100, 142. *See also*
  Excretory system
Water (H_2O). *See also* Atmosphere;
  Evaporation; Fresh water;
  Groundwater; Lakes; Oceans;
  Rivers; Soil moisture; Water
  molecule
  amount of Earth's, 219, 220
  in atmosphere, 220
  as cell resource, 86
  for cell survival, 95
  and cellular respiration, 119
  defined, 142
  effect on temperatures, 232
  food for cells, 100
  free, 220
  fresh, 219, 220, 248, 251, 256
  in human body, 60
  on Mars, 151
  mixtures of, 6
  need for, 221
  nitrogen and oxygen in, 185
  as one of four properties of, 42
  one of six nutrient groups, 120
  origin, 219–220, 248
  particles, 25
  and photosynthesis, 115–117,
    131–132
  plants make sugar from sunshine,
    carbon dioxide, and, 103, 116
  as product in chemical reaction, 33
  salt, 220, 248, 251, 258
  surface, 220
  underground, 220
  to underground roots, 102

use, 221–222
  as variable, 112, 113
  and xylem system, 109
Water cycle
  defined, 260
  description of, 223–224
  effect on weather patterns, 251
  and recycling, 248
  role of ocean in California weather,
    235
  Sun as driver of, 224
  water evaporation from Earth's
    surface, 224–225
  water falls back to Earth's surface,
    225–226
Water map of California, 246–247
Water molecule. *See also* Water
  defined, 183–184, 194, 260
  representation of, 184–185
  and water vapor, 194–195, 225–226
Water planet, 219–222. *See also* Earth
Water vapor. *See also* Condensation
  and clouds, 234
  and condensation, 189–195
  defined, 183, 260
  and evaporation, 183–184, 225–226
  and free molecule, 185
  and humidity, 197
  in hurricanes and tropical storms, 229
  liquid water changed to, 224
  made of individual water molecules,
    194–195, 225–226
  rainwater reentering atmosphere as,
    226
  satellite images of, 239
  and saturation, 186
  and thunderstorms, 230
  and warm front, 240
  in water cycle, 248
Weather. *See also* Air; Severe weather; *and
  entries for specific types of weather*
  and atmospheric pressure, 213
  changes in, 207
  defined, 228, 260
  hot and cold, 232
  role of ocean in California, 234–235

290